Kindred Hearts

Also by Debra Evans

The Complete Book on Childbirth
The Mystery of Womanhood
Heart and Home
Fragrant Offerings
Beauty for Ashes
Without Moral Limits
Blessed Events
Preparing for Childbirth
The Woman's Complete Guide to Personal Health Care
Beauty and the Best
Christian Parenting Answers (General Editor)
Women of Character

Kindred Hearts

Nurturing the Bond Between
Mother & Daughter

Debra Evans

PUBLISHING
Colorado Springs, Colorado

KINDRED HEARTS

Copyright © 1997 by Debra Evans
All rights reserved. International copyright secured.

Library of Congress Cataloging-in-Publication Data
Evans, Debra.
    Kindred hearts : Nurturing the bond between mother and daughter / Debra Evans.
      p.   cm.
    ISBN 1-56179-437-6
    1. Mothers and daughters.   2. Parenting—Religious aspects—Christianity.
I. Title.
HQ755.85.E96   1997
306.874'3—dc21   96-49096
                                                              CIP

Published by Focus on the Family Publishing, Colorado Springs, Colorado 80995

Distributed in the U.S.A. and Canada by Word Books, Dallas, Texas

Unless otherwise noted, Scripture quotations are from THE HOLY BIBLE, NEW INTER-NATIONAL VERSION ® . Copyright © 1973, 1978, 1984 by the International Bible Society. Used by permission of Zondervan Publishing House. All rights reserved. Quotations identified as NASB are from the *New American Standard Bible,* © 1960, 1963, 1968, 1971, 1973, 1975, 1977 by The Lockman Foundation. Used by permission. Quotations identified as TLB are from *The Living Bible,* © 1971. Used by permission of Tyndale House Publishers, Inc., Wheaton, IL 60189. All rights reserved. Quotations identified as KJV are from the King James Version. Quotations identified as J. B. Phillips are from J. B. Phillips, *The New Testament in Modern English for Schools,* New Revised Edition (London: William Collins Sons and Co. Ltd., 1972). Copyright © 1959, 1960, 1972 by J. B. Phillips. Quotations identified as NEB are from the *New English Bible,* © 1961, 1970 by the Delegates of the Oxford University Press and the Syndics of the Cambridge University Press.

Some names and certain details of case studies mentioned in this book have been changed to protect the privacy of the individuals involved.

Focus on the Family books are available at special quantity discounts when purchased in bulk by corporations, organizations, churches, or groups. Special imprints, messages, and excerpts can be produced to meet your needs. For more information, contact: Sales Dept., Focus on the Family Publishing, 8605 Explorer Dr., Colorado Springs, CO 80920; or phone (719) 531-3400.

Editor: Michele A. Kendall

Cover Design: BC Studios

Printed in the United States of America

97 98 99 00 01 02 03/10 9 8 7 6 5 4 3 2 1

To my two incomparably talented daughters,
Joanna Elizabeth and Katherine Laurel,
who fill my heart with joy
and bless my life with their tender friendship.
I thank God for the precious gift of *you*—
and for making me your mother.
Love always, Mom

Contents

Acknowledgments

As with children, books are born in stages, and I am especially thankful for the kind assistance of those who made the delivery of *Kindred Hearts* a particularly satisfying adventure:

my faithful contingent of survey participants, who sent in their wonderfully detailed replies from across the United States and beyond—because of your timely help, this book sings loud and clear, and the chorus of voices it contains will tell many women that they aren't alone in their mother-daughter experiences;

my mother, Nancy Allen Munger, who graciously provided her permission for me to share part of our story;

my daughters, Joanna and Katherine, who were willing to let me share sensitive areas of our lives and listened without criticism;

my granddaughter, Abigail, for reminding me every day how blessed I am;

my sisters, Kerry Olson and Nancy Shallow, who have helped me process the past and look ahead with joy to the future;

my friends Elaine Hucklebridge, Katherine Bennett, Merry Nell Drummond, and Barb Pett, who encouraged me along the way;

my mentor, Tryn Clark, whose example of spiritual mothering has been a treasured source of inspiration for nearly two decades;

my women's Bible study group—most notably, co-leaders Tina Nagel and Janine Garrett—and our pastor, Will Davis Jr., whose consistent teaching of God's Word brings renewal, refreshment, and reasons to keep running the race wholeheartedly;

my director of publishing at Focus on the Family, Al Janssen, for providing a place for the vision to become a reality;

my first editor, Gwen Weising, who planted the idea and helped me believe that the words would follow;

my new editor, Michele Kendall, for calmly easing the transition after Gwen's departure with delightful expertise, then pressing for excellence and polishing the final version until it glowed;

my editorial, marketing, and design and production teams, especially Betsy Reinheimer, Bonnie Horning, Mike Leming, Connie Carleton, and BC Studios, whose careful attention to the creative details honors the King you diligently serve;

my agents, Mike Hyatt and Robert Wolgemuth, because you know what you're doing and accomplish your tasks so well;

my father, John Munger, for quietly remaining true to your beliefs and not leaving when things got tough;

my sons, David and Jon, whose continuing growth cheers my heart;

and, as always, my husband, Dave, who spent many hours hearing about my concerns, ideas, frustrations, dreams, heartaches, and hypotheses—and knew just when I most needed a hug, a back rub, or a prayer.

For those whose names, for brevity's sake, are not listed here, please know I have not forgotten your patient support and skillful service. My life has been enriched in manifold ways through the time and labor we have shared.

To all of these dear friends, colleagues, advisers, and family members, I say thank you. May the Lord, who is the lasting source of your hope and confidence, continually strengthen you for the work He has uniquely created and equipped you to do. To God be the glory!

From Generation to Generation

Mother love makes a woman more vulner-
able than any other creature on earth.

—*Pam Brown*

Chapter One

Something wasn't right. Though she was only 11 years old, Emily knew that her mother needed help. *Her* help.

If I can just be good enough, maybe Mom won't get so angry at Dad. Maybe if I keep getting good grades, it will make life easier for all of us. And if I make some of her favorite cookies, Mom might forget about being mad and smile a little.

Emily, an A student and talented flute player, could not understand why her mother and father were arguing so often, and she blamed herself for the angry outbursts her mom usually directed her way following a fight.

One evening, as Emily sat at her desk preparing for the next day's math exam, her mother walked into her bedroom without knocking, her face flushed with anger.

"You forgot to clean up your mess in the bathroom again, Emily!" she shouted.

"But, Mom, I'm studying for tomorrow's test." Emily recoiled from her mother's accusing words. Stifling a sob, she added, "I'm sorry I left my things out. I'll clean everything up as soon as I finish this chapter."

Twenty minutes later, Emily headed toward the bathroom. It was 10:15 P.M. Everyone was in bed, and the house was quiet.

I've got to do a better job straightening things up around here. Mom has a hard enough time without me adding to her problems, Emily thought as she collected the cleaning supplies from the hall closet. *Why does she get so mad at me all the time? She must really hate me.*

With no apologies offered from her mother to soothe her hurt, Emily was left to absorb her mother's pain as she proceeded to scrub the sink, tub, and toilet, clean the mirror and counter, and empty the trashcan. Half an hour later, the bathroom was spotless. Reaching for her toothbrush, the young girl looked into the mirror and burst into tears.

Fourteen years later, when Emily was expecting her first child, this almost-forgotten scene from her childhood was vividly revived with the smell of glass cleaner being applied to a smudged window by a waiter. Instantly, Emily's breath caught at the back of her throat. A familiar sadness welled up inside her, causing her to momentarily close her eyes.

"What's wrong, Em?" her husband, Greg, asked gently. They were sitting in a vinyl-covered booth at a local restaurant. Greg reached for her hand across the table.

"I'll be okay. Don't worry about me. Go ahead and finish eating," Emily said, slowly stroking her pregnant belly.

"Is it about your mom?"

"Yes, it is. How did you guess?"

"By the look on your face," Greg explained.

Downplaying her rising emotional turmoil, Emily smiled and said half-jokingly, "You know what they say about pregnant women's mood swings resembling a roller coaster." Turning serious, she added, "I certainly seem to be thinking a lot about my childhood lately. Mom can still get to me, can't she? You know, I really hated it when she used to shout at me. And usually I hadn't done anything wrong!"

Suddenly, Emily looked straight into her husband's eyes. "Greg, *I am not like my mother*. I'm not going to treat this child the way Mom treated me. I love our baby too much."

"You don't have to convince me of that, honey. I think you're going to be a fantastic mother. Look at the way you've taken care of yourself since you found out you're pregnant. You eat only healthy, low-fat foods, do all of your prenatal exercises, and practice your breathing techniques every day. You've probably read every parenting book the library owns. And you pray enough for both of us."

Noticing that his wife's attention had started to drift, Greg paused.

"Are you listening to what I'm saying, Emily?"

"Sorry. My mind was on something else. Weren't you just talking about what a good mom you think I'm going to be?"

When the baby arrived five months later, her birth stirred up a surprising blend of feelings within Emily's heart. Overcome with a sense of awe that the joining of two tiny cells had resulted in her eight-pound baby, Emily smiled as tears of joy and relief trickled down her cheeks.

Birth is a bittersweet event, Emily found—a place where heaven and earth collide in a perplexing clash of hopes, dreams, facts, fears, questions, and expectations.

Before becoming a mother I had a hundred theories on how to bring up children. Now I have seven children and only one theory: love them, especially when they least deserve to be loved.
—KATE SAMPERI

———— ❧ ————

Cast all your anxiety on him because he cares for you.
—1 PETER 5:7

———— ❧ ————

There is nothing more thrilling in this world, I think, than having a child that is yours, and yet is mysteriously a stranger.
—AGATHA CHRISTIE

———— ❧ ————

"When my first child was born, I finally believed that my mother saw me as an adult. We became more equal."
—PENNY, AGE 44

Someday, she would face another, distinctly different kind of separation when her daughter reached adulthood and left home to experience life on her own.

Emily wrapped the baby up and snuggled her close. *What kind of person will you grow up to be?* she thought as she stroked her daughter's silky cheek. She could only trust in God and time to bring the answers.

"Yes, yes, here I am, my sweet baby. There's no need to cry. Shhh . . . there, there now," Emily whispered soothingly. "Everything's all right. Here I am."

The word *mother* was too new a term for her to apply to herself yet. Perhaps in a few days, or weeks, the title would fit more comfortably.

Suddenly, an unwelcome helplessness swept over Emily. The baby in her arms, so small and defenseless, called forth feelings she had never experienced with any other human being, prompting her to voice a silent prayer—the first of many that Emily would offer to God on Courtney's behalf over the coming years.

Father, I praise You for this precious gift! Help me to be a loving mother. I thank You for loaning her to me. Please help me nurture and protect her. She belongs to You, Lord. Shield her from harm and evil. Please make her a shining witness of Your glory and grace. I pray in Jesus' name. Amen.

Suddenly, there was a knock at the birthing-room door, signaling an expected guest's arrival.

"Come in," Greg called out. He hadn't stopped grinning from the moment his precious newborn had entered the world.

"Where is my adorable new granddaughter?" the excited grandmother whispered, correctly sensing that any loud talk would disturb the magnificence of the moment.

As her mother bent down to kiss her on the cheek, Emily smiled warmly and extended her hand.

New Beginnings

"There is nothing on earth like the moment of seeing one's first baby," affirmed Katherine Trevelyan. "Men scale other heights, but there is no height like this simple one, occurring continuously throughout all the ages in musty bedrooms, in palaces, in caves and desert places."

Speaking for many of us, she added, "I looked at this rolled-up bundle . . . and knew again I had not created her. She was herself apart from me. She had her own life to lead, her own destiny to accomplish; she just came past me to this earth. My job was to get her to adulthood and then push her off."[1]

The scene is repeated each day, with countless variations, as mothers the world over begin nurturing daughters entrusted to their care and protection. To each of us, a daughter's arrival represents a new beginning, the first step on the mother-daughter journey, a fresh start. It also presents a second chance to work things through with our own mothers as we encounter family life from a changed perspective—it's a chance to better understand the past and, ultimately, to forgive.

From the womb to the grave, a daughter's identity is intimately interwoven with her mother's, blending together the vivid life-patterns of two distinctly separate and unique individuals. For some women, there is ample reason to rejoice in this truth; for others, it is an inescapable reminder of a past they would prefer to forget. Either way, it doesn't alter our responsibility for raising strong and capable daughters—women who, with God's help, will someday find and fulfill their unique calling as we are finding and fulfilling ours today.

One of the first things we discover about mothering is that we cannot control many things in our

You have to love your children unselfishly. That's hard. But it's the only way.
—BARBARA BUSH

—— ❧ ——

For you created my inmost being; you knit me together in my mother's womb.
—PSALM 139:13

—— ❧ ——

We cannot insist that the first years of infancy are of supreme importance, and that mothers are not of supreme importance.
—G. K. CHESTERTON

—— ❧ ——

Simplicity is the secret of seeing things clearly.
—OSWALD CHAMBERS

—— ❧ ——

From the mouth of infants and nursing babes Thou hast established strength.
—PSALM 8:2, NASB

children's lives. Our daughters entered a fallen world when they were born, just as we did. Even if our mothers did a fantastic, first-rate job raising us, preparing us well for motherhood, that doesn't alter the fact that dramatic changes in family life have taken place during the past 30 years. Our children face cultural, political, social, and spiritual challenges—and opportunities—that would horrify and amaze yesterday's grandmothers. However much we would like to turn back the clock to an earlier era and act as if our daughters aren't living in troublesome times, we can't do that, because they are. And we need to build strong bonds between us to weather the storms.

Isn't it a welcome relief to know we can help our daughters grow up to place their faith in God, even though we don't know what their futures hold? We can't create their faith for them—but we *can* give our daughters a remarkable range of spiritual strategies for confronting and coping with life's challenges; we can't totally predict the final outcome of our long years of mothering—but we *can* point and guide our daughters in the right direction. Mothering a daughter is a rigorous occupation, and the way we raise our daughters is influenced by our pasts and drawn forth by our futures. We learn as we go. We all make mistakes. We sometimes feel inadequate for the task. Yet the secret of building a healthy mother-daughter bond may be less complicated than many of us realize.

A Lasting Legacy

Our mothers play a powerful part in our lives. Like it or not, for better or worse, our mothers make an immutable imprint on the core of our beings by showing us in countless tangible and intangible ways, from the moment we are born, what it means to be a woman. And we, in turn, will have the same impact on our daughters.

We arrive—in a state of total helplessness and carrying an inborn need to be loved, cherished, affirmed, and nurtured—without first being asked our opinion about who our mothers should be. Whether the mother-daughter relationship is initiated by childbirth, remarriage, or adoption is really beside the point. Becoming the mother of a daughter—by any means, wherever and whenever it happens—is an unforgettable, humbling, life-changing experience.

Now, here we are, our mothers' daughters, having become mothers to daughters of our own. Like Emily, we know our daughters' lives hold tremendous potential. And, as most of our mothers did before us, we want to raise them to the best of our ability. What will our legacy be?

Standing at the crossroads between two generations, we are indelibly marked by the past as we head into an unknown future—wondering what we can do differently, deciding what to do the same, keeping the beliefs and traditions we agree with, discarding those we don't agree with. Our mothers, in a sense, go with us on this journey. Whether they are still living or have died, their influence continues to have a profound impact on who we are, how we think, and what we do.

By picking up *Kindred Hearts*, you have chosen to take a fresh look at the bonds you share with your mother and daughter. You appreciate the importance of your role as the living link placed between three successive generations of women. You know firsthand, as I do, that these feminine family ties are among the most lovely, influential, frustrating, fulfilling, difficult, joyous, heartrending, extraordinary, temperamental, and life-enhancing relationships you will experience. Whether you're a brand-new mom, the mother of an adolescent, or, like me, the grandmother of a grown daughter's daughter, you under-

I never thought that you should be rewarded for the greatest privilege of life.
—MAY ROPER COKER, ON BEING CHOSEN MOTHER OF THE YEAR, 1958

One mother achieves more than a hundred teachers.
—JEWISH PROVERB

"With what she had to work with, my mother did the best she could."
—RUTH, AGE 42

Teach me to do your will, for you are my God; may your good Spirit lead me on level ground.
—PSALM 143:10

stand that your words, actions, and prayers leave a lasting impression upon loved ones God places in your life. In reading this book, it is my hope that you will receive encouragement as you consider the emotional and spiritual significance of the irreplaceable connection you share.

Here we are, you and I, appointed to the humble-yet-powerful position of ministering to women and girls both older and younger, more seasoned and less experienced, and slower and quicker than we, the kindred hearts we have cherished (and perhaps clashed with) from the time of our first meeting. If it were up to us, regardless of what our family histories have been, we would elect that everything between us would go well from this day forward. We pray tomorrow will be even better than yesterday.

Go for It!

My reason for writing *Kindred Hearts* is not because I'm a national expert on the subject of human relationships (I'm not!), or because I can look back on mothering my own two daughters over the past 25 years and report that our family experiences have always been problem-free (I can't!). I wrote these chapters because I want to cheer you on in strengthening the bonds the Lord has given to you, to say "Go for it!" as loudly and clearly as I can, to stand with you in affirming the matchless value of your family roles, and to let you know that change is possible if you are willing to face difficult areas, asking God for His help, mercy, and direction.

In speaking with my friends and many of the moms in the classes, seminars, and women's conferences I've taught over the years, what I hear women say repeatedly is that they want to experience satisfying, strong relationships with their daughters and mothers. Each woman I have talked with has expressed an inner desire to be loved by her mother and to develop a loving bond with her daughter. But many women report experiencing numerous difficulties that have undermined or damaged these primary relationships.

A Chorus of Voices

What actually strengthens or weakens the mother-daughter bond? Are there any common truths we can apply in building our relationships? How can we best nurture the bond we share with our daughters and mothers as they confront life's daily pressures?

As I asked myself these questions while doing research for this book, I decided to send out 200 surveys to women across the country, asking them to share some specific ways their moms contributed to, or took away from, the vitality of their bond. When I got the surveys back, what surprised me most about the women's responses was how clearly they described a number of key elements that help create a satisfying, or dissatisfying, mother-daughter relationship. The surveys turned out to be the most valuable—and convincing—part of my research; I ended up using what I learned from the women who participated in it throughout the entire book. A number of the stories women shared in the surveys are included in later chapters as well, and although people's names and other identifying details have been disguised to preserve confidentiality, all of the accounts you will read are presumed to be true.

Some Final Words

I pray that as you consider what these women have said and complete the exercises in *Kindred Hearts*, you will take what you need from each chapter and leave the rest behind, creatively adapting whatever you deem useful to your own one-of-a-kind situa-

Judicious mothers will always keep in mind that they are the first book read, and the last put aside, in every child's library.
—C. LENOX REDMOND

—— ❧ ——

What a wonder it is— this miracle that happens every day and every hour! Only, the unusual strikes us more. God is always doing wonders.
—GEORGE MACDONALD, IN RESPONSE TO HIS DAUGHTER CAROLINE'S BIRTH

—— ❧ ——

There is no [human] influence so powerful as that of the mother.
—SARAH JOSEPHA HALE

tion. In writing these pages, I have tried to picture you reading them, scribbling along the edges as I would, turning to passages of Scripture that God calls to your mind, realizing that what you read here about mother-daughter relationships is not so much something new that you are learning as something you know already in your heart and are thankful to be reminded of.

Your Personal Mother-Daughter Mailbox

Using separate pieces of paper, write three letters—one to your mother, one to yourself, and one to your daughter. This exercise is intended to help you identify and express your thoughts and feelings to, and for, no one but yourself. Since these letters are for your eyes only, you have the freedom to write whatever you like because they will not be read by anyone but you.

NOTE: Completing this exercise before you read any of the upcoming chapters may bring you greater benefit as you consider the topics that follow, but if writing these letters brings up painful memories, please take time to pray before resuming the exercise. You may want to come back to it *after* reading later chapters.

IF YOU DO NOT HAVE A DAUGHTER: After you have finished writing the first letter to your mother, write a second letter to yourself about your goals and aspirations, fears and anxieties, and hopes and dreams regarding parenthood.

LETTER #1: Tell your mother how you feel about the way she raised you. Think back to specific moments when she said or did something, for better or worse, that proved to have a lasting impact on your life. Be as descriptive as possible. What role did your mother play in shaping your opinion of yourself? Your values? Your likes and dislikes? Your talents and career choices? Finally, share with your mother about what you most appreciate receiving from her—and what you would like to say to her to affirm and bless her in return.

LETTER #2: Reflect upon the years you have spent mothering your daughter and what the relationship has meant to you. Record your favorite highlights and greatest concerns. Are there any areas that need extra attention? Would you like to be doing anything differently? Describe your daughter's unique personality, temperament, and talents, her likes and dislikes, and your hopes for her future. Now give yourself a pat on the back: Write a few words that will bring you comfort and encouragement for a job well done and for the years ahead.

LETTER #3: In this letter, focus your thoughts and words not on who you would like your daughter to be in the future, but on who she is today. Tell her about when she was born (or adopted) and how you felt. Assure your daughter of your deep desire to cherish and protect her God-given attributes and abilities. What is it about her that makes her truly one-of-a-kind? What are your hopes for her? Above all, tell your daughter about your love for her, your pleasure connected with sharing her life's journey, and your joy in watching her grow up to become the woman God created her to be.

What's the Secret?

Other things may change us, but we start and end with the family.

—Anthony Brandt

Chapter Two

*L*ast night, I went for a walk through the neighborhood with my 24-year-old daughter, Joanna.
We started out slowly, but by the third block, the
pace had picked up. I was especially pleased when Joanna
noticed that my fitness level had increased significantly since our
last hike. We chatted and compared notes about our day, as
crickets and cicadas chirruped around us.

Then Joanna said, "Mom, you take more steps and have
shorter strides than I do. My legs are a *lot* longer than yours!"

I had not noticed this before, but Joanna was right: My feet
were hitting the pavement much more frequently than hers were.

Joanna's casual comment wasn't about her attempt to imitate,
or even compete with, me. It was a simple statement of fact.
Though we had adjusted our pace to match one another's, our

strides were surprisingly out of sync. I found it comforting to know we could walk together in spite of our contrasting styles.

Suddenly, memories of walking beside my mother as a little girl rushed back to me. I remembered trying to match Mom's far-apart steps as my small legs scurried to keep up, and I remembered how impossibly long her legs looked. No matter how hard I worked at it, I could not stretch my stride to equal my mother's; when I made my steps bigger, I was forced to go even more slowly.

Forty years later, I could clearly recall my childish attempt to exactly copy my mom on several occasions—the towering figure with a womanly way of walking whom I desperately wanted to imitate. Now I was the mother with a grown daughter walking beside me, comparing her gait with mine.

Later in the evening, just as I was drifting off to sleep, thoughts about our evening walk returned to me with a new focus. When Joanna was a baby, she could not walk; I carried her. During her toddler years, I alternately waited for her teetering steps to steady, then scrambled after her if she decided to engage in a sudden sprint. With each passing year, I awkwardly learned to readjust my pace to my daughter's, which at times tested the limits of my endurance—especially during her adolescence, when Joanna preferred not to walk with me at all. (She claimed that her cheerleader status demanded intense aerobic workouts, but I suspect she also thought that going for a leisurely stroll with Mom around the neighborhood was just plain boring.)

These days, I am delighted—and relieved—that we can walk together once again. It took many years to reach our easily shared pace.

Joanna cannot remember when she could not walk; she cannot look back on her early slow-paced months and smile with me at each eye-popping milestone: the day she turned over for the first time; her initial attempts at crawling and creeping; the repeated tumbles on the carpet by the couch after she had pulled herself up to a standing position; those earliest, teetering steps when I clapped and cheered and cried at her energetic efforts. And she cannot understand yet what it was like for me to curb my well-cultivated, watchful maternal gait as she asked for the car keys for the first time, ran to the family station wagon, and backed out of the driveway in a triumphant blaze of teen glory.

But *I* can look back and remember, and though Joanna often does not realize it, I am still adjusting my stride to hers.

A Study in Contrasts

Isn't this a significant part of what mothering our daughters is all about? I have never met a mother whose daughter's way of "walking"—the sum of her singular mannerisms, opinions, idiosyncrasies, habits, temperament, heart attitudes, talents, beliefs, and abilities—exactly matches her mother's. And who doesn't at times struggle with these differences?

I am firmly convinced that mothers who share healthy relationships with their daughters set a pace that is sensitive to and supportive of their daughters' developmental strides. It is not our daughters' responsibility to perform the necessary pacemaking adjustments during most of our lifelong journey together—it is ours. And our daughters greatly benefit from our boundary-setting rate of speed.

If we received a legacy of loving affirmation, consistent discipline, appropriate physical nurturing, and genuine protection from our mothers, we were provided a head start. For those of us who were not given these things, we should not be surprised when we feel as if we are heading into unfamiliar territory or lagging behind our better-prepared peers.

Be not angry that you cannot make others as you wish them to be, since you cannot make yourself as you wish to be.
—THOMAS À KEMPIS

When the way is rough, your patience has a chance to grow. So let it grow. . . . For when your patience is finally in full bloom, then you will be ready for anything, strong in character, full and complete.
—JAMES 1:3–4, TLB

Only in growth, reform, and change, paradoxically enough, is true security to be found.
—ANNE MORROW LINDBERGH

"My mom has a wonderful way of being at home with anyone."
—VONDA, AGE 38

Regardless of what kind of "road training" our past histories and backgrounds brought into our lives, there are times when we may find it difficult to know how, when, and where to guide the mother-daughter relationship. We may assume that we are not good mothers if our daughters depart from the course we want them to follow. And we may take it personally when our daughters reject our way of doing things.

"It wasn't until Danielle was about seven years old that I started to feel panic-stricken at times about my mothering ability," a 34-year-old mother named Karen told me recently. "Her needs were so different from what they had been before she started going to school all day. Rather than enjoying our one-on-one time, I felt irritated by her constant questions and need to be near me. But I was most bothered by my own feelings of inadequacy as a mother.

"When I noticed how shy and withdrawn Danielle was compared with other girls her age, I immediately thought, *If I had done things differently, if I had been a better mother, my daughter wouldn't be acting like this.*"

I believe that Karen's initial reaction to her daughter's emerging social skills is a common one. The familiar refrain begins *If I can just be a good enough mother . . .* and then goes on to outline all of the wonderful and amazing things our daughters will be capable of doing and becoming as a result of our impressive mothering skills.

This desire to be a "good enough" mother places incredible pressure on us. The result is that we feel guilty, inadequate, frustrated, angry, or depressed when these unrealistic messages about motherhood end in "failure." Consciously or unconsciously, we make our daughters the measure of our own success as mothers. But when we lock ourselves into impossible-to-fulfill expectations and rigid perfectionism, we never really get to know our daughters, just as many of our mothers never got to know us. We know only our ideal of them.

Side-by-side travel across the changing seasons of our lives requires us to abandon this troublesome way of thinking—for good.

What Women Say Builds Up—and Tears Down— the Mother-Daughter Bond

Given our differences, how do we best build a relationship with our growing daughters that recognizes, honors, and protects their God-given uniqueness?

I think that, in part, the answer to this question lies in what adult daughters say they received—or wished they had received—as a lasting legacy from their mothers. These women can look back with clarity and poignantly define how their moms developed or denied them a sense of well-being within the relationship.

When asked what they especially liked about their moms, women with stable, satisfying mother-daughter relationships said the following:

> *"My mom was always supportive of me. During times when I know she disapproved, she still gave me every measure of support. I always felt her love for me was unconditional."*
>
> —Bonnie, age 42

> *"Mom gave me her total support! She never belittled me or made me feel unworthy."*
>
> —Ronda, age 31

> *"I always felt loved. She listened and offered closeness and companionship."*
>
> —Ann, no age given

Anything which parents have not learned from experience, they can now learn from their children.
—ANONYMOUS

— ❧ —

Children are likely to live up to what you believe of them.
—LADY BIRD JOHNSON

— ❧ —

She is just an extraordinary mother and a gentle person. I depended on her for everything. . . . I watched her become a strong person, and that had an enormous influence on me.
—ROSALYNN CARTER

— ❧ —

It is by loving and not by being loved that one can come nearest the soul of another.
—GEORGE MACDONALD

"My mother loved me and she gave her best to see me progress and develop in life."

—Evelyn, age 51

"Mom and I are very close. I respect and appreciate her—I genuinely enjoy her and have fun times with her. She models a real and close walk with Christ."

—Kelli, age 24

"She never gave up on me, no matter what I did or said. She loved me unconditionally!"

—Melissa, age 20

"My mom is my friend, my confidante—someone I can laugh with, a person who prays for me. I am very rich."

—Janet, age 51

"She was so good about encouraging me to do anything I wanted to do."

—Meg, age 48

"My mom has always, always supported me and encouraged my individuality. She respects and trusts and loves me unconditionally. My mom was a spiritual example in my life. Now that I'm grown, Mom is everything I could want her to be."

—Kristin, age 21

"Mom has always been available when I've needed to talk. She shows me a lot of love and attention and has always encouraged me. Mom makes me feel that I can succeed and that I have her support."

—Julie, age 25

"I knew that she loved me no matter what."
—Marcie, age 44

On the other hand, women who have experienced strained or fractured mother-daughter relationships told me:

"My mom didn't nurture me or help me to know that I was special."
—Theresa, age 40

"I felt like she wanted me to be someone I wasn't."
—Kathy, age 21

"I didn't have a mom that took time to share in my life. I felt like I was always an inconvenience to her."
—Colleen, age 31

"I didn't have Mom's personal attention or the general feeling of being taken care of."
—Anna, age 34

"We don't have a real relationship—a friendship. My mom isn't someone I can confide in and share my life experiences with, someone who would support me in life experiences other than school activities."
—Tiki, age 21

"My mom took my mistakes as a reflection on herself, rather than realizing that 'kids will be kids.' She was constantly upset and worried about her 'image.'"
—SARAH, AGE 26

———— ⅋ ————

I looked on child rearing not only as a work of love and duty but as a profession that was fully as interesting and challenging as any honorable profession in the world and one that demanded the best that I could bring to it.
—ROSE KENNEDY

———— ⅋ ————

When asked what they would change about their moms, many survey participants answered: "I wish that my mom fully accepted and supported me."

"Sincerity. Compassion. Nonjudgmental advice/responses. Patience. Ability to listen and hear. These are the things that I wanted that I didn't have in my mom."

—Tina, age 31

"I wanted my mom to be someone who would love me and desire to know me; she never loved, she only criticized."

—Gail, age 42

"I would have liked to have a mother who showed an active interest in my personal achievements, who affirmed me, who contributed to my children's growth."

—Win, age 60

"Mom didn't love me affectionately or tell me she loved me. I would have liked it if she had made me feel special. (I was the oldest of two boys and two girls.)"

—Linda, age 42

"My mother was/is very critical, outspoken, and insensitive."

—Carol, age 39

"I didn't have a mom who took the time to get to know me and love me for my uniqueness. She always wanted me to be different."

—Emily, age 35

This is not theoretical, ivory tower research gleaned from textbooks. It is what women identify as the essential, boiled-down, real-life ingredients that go into making or breaking the mother-daughter bond.

Taken together, these honest, heartfelt responses open a window through which we glimpse a dynamic truth: A healthy mother-daughter relationship is built by loving one's daughter for the person God uniquely created her to be; honoring her with time, attention, and affection; and giving her to God for His purposes and glory.

Many "add-ons," such as similar interests, shared beliefs, and spiritual support, serve to enrich this bond, of course. But women report that a mutually rewarding mother-daughter relationship can exist even without these things.

Growing in Grace

"My mom and I are incredibly different," shared Diana. "She likes Mozart, I can't stand classical music. I prefer wearing nice clothes, she's always in blue jeans. She rarely turns on the television, I watch several weekly shows and tape them when I'm away for the evening. I'm talkative, she's quiet. There have been times in my life when her mannerisms have irritated me so much, I thought there would never be common ground between us beyond our faith in Christ. But we've worked through our differences to the point where we enjoy spending time together. My mom feels secure about herself. She doesn't shut me out when I criticize or tease her."

After listening to her daughter's summary, Diana's mom, Marcie, grinned and said with mock seriousness, "It's true. Diana and I probably couldn't be any more different than we are. Though it took me a number of years to realize it, I now know, beyond a shadow of a doubt, that I gave birth to an updated version of my mother-in-law when I had Diana."

Then, giving her daughter a big hug, Marcie

For me, a line from my mother is more efficacious than all the homilies preached in Lent.
—HENRY WADSWORTH LONGFELLOW

—— ✑ ——

In motherhood there's so much to learn, so much to give, and although the learning gets less with each child, the giving never does.
—MARGUERITE KELLY

—— ✑ ——

We should love those who point out our faults, but we seldom do.
—ANONYMOUS

—— ✑ ——

A mother understands what a child does not say.
—JEWISH PROVERB

—— ✑ ——

Each heart knows its own bitterness, and no one else can share its joy.
—PROVERBS 14:10

smiled and added, "And, yes, I really, really, really *do* love my mother-in-law!"

Are you and your daughter, like Marcie and Diana, faced with striking differences in your personalities, outlooks, demeanor, and opinions, or are you surprisingly similar? Where are you in your relationship with your daughter? How has your relationship changed over the years? In what ways are you adjusting your stride to hers as you build and strengthen your relationship?

Be encouraged: No matter how much time you have invested in building the bond you share with your daughter, you can improve your relationship in the weeks and months ahead by reading this book, applying its end-of-the-chapter activities, and taking time to reflect upon what you learn. Gracefully maintaining your sense of humor—for the rest of your life—won't hurt either.

Mom's Message Board

Is there anything you would like to say to your daughter as a result of reading this chapter? Use this space to record your thoughts, and share your message with her later.

Shared Reflections

The precursor of the mirror is the mother's face.

—D. W. Winnicott

Chapter Three

————— ⸎ —————

*L*ong before we discovered mirrors and pho-
tographs, our mothers' reflections provided us
with the earliest glimpses of our female identity. Gazing up from the familiar enclosure of Mother's arms,
what did we see?

Were we greeted often with acceptance and joy, tears and
laughter, the soothing reassurance that all was well? Did exhaustion, anxiety, and a sense of helplessness occasionally obscure the
view? Was our appearance welcomed? What did the sound of
our mothers' voices and their touch tell us?

Mothers are the first mirrors in which we see ourselves
reflected. From this relationship, we gain our initial impressions
of what it means to have been created in God's image as a
female—and how to *be* a female. Our mothers' body language,
speech, and eye contact produce primary pictures in the portrait

gallery of our self-images. The bond we share produces the foundation of our identities and our first feelings about ourselves, and gives us our earliest lessons about whether the world is a secure or a shaky place to live.

Looking back on the first days of my granddaughter Abigail's life, I can clearly recall my amazement concerning my daughter's caring for her baby in the neonatal intensive care unit (NICU) at an Atlanta-area children's hospital. The high-tech, brightly lit room with buzzers and beepers repeatedly going off should have intimidated Joanna. But it took my daughter only a few minutes to overcome her preliminary fear of that stress-filled place. Within moments after the baby's arrival, her mom was caring for her: stroking, cooing, praying, loving. The fact that Abigail had been born with spina bifida, a complex birth defect involving the central nervous system, did not stop Joanna from providing a sense of security for her, even in the midst of a medical crisis.

It was a less-than-perfect introduction to mothering. In fact, it was one of those times when you hang on for dear life and pray to God for His strength and grace to see you through, when joy and sadness flow together in a disorienting emotional mixture that seems to turn your whole world upside down in a matter of seconds: the birth of a first child . . . the news of the diagnosis . . . the baby's need to be nurtured by a mom who was simultaneously celebrating the arrival of her precious one and grieving over the surgeries her little girl must endure . . . the newborn daughter looking into the mirror of her mother's face.

It is an imperfect world, and we cannot love our daughters perfectly. We are not able to prevent pain and sin from entering their lives. We do not know what the outcome of many years of multilevel investment in our daughters' lives will be. We come from flawed families, and sometimes, without thinking, we do or say the very things we promised ourselves we would never do or say.

Even so, when I think of 21-year-old Joanna standing quietly beside Abigail's isolette in the NICU, when I remember the faces of the thousands of mothers I have worked with over the years in expectant-parent classes, when I recall snuggling my daughter Katherine in my arms and kissing the soft skin on her forehead, then the apostle Paul's words about living as Christians in a groaning world gently rise to the surface of my memory: "And we know that in all things God works for the good of those who love him, who have been called according to his purpose. . . . [N]either death nor life, neither angels nor demons, neither the present nor the future, nor any powers, neither height nor depth, nor anything else in all creation, will be able to separate us from the love of God that is in Christ Jesus our Lord" (Rom. 8:28,38–39).

Mothering, like life, is an exhilarating, exhausting, learn-as-you-go, roller-coaster ride of an experience. And it is comforting to know that God is riding up and down over the bumpy tracks with us.

When They Look in the Mirror, What Do They See?

Our daughters, from the moment they arrive in our lives, look to us to "mirror" information back to them about who they are. The accuracy of our reflections depends a great deal on our ability to see them clearly, as separate and unique individuals entrusted to us by God for nurturing and protection until they reach adulthood. It is also considerably affected by the type and quality of the bond we shared with our own mothers.

Imagine for a moment what it would be like to live as a young child in a house where the only

The proper nourishment for personal growth is a loving acceptance and encouragement by others, not rejection and impatient suggestions for improvement.
—JOHN POWELL

We should measure affection not by the ardor of its passion, but by its strength and constancy.
—CICERO

A close-knit and loving home is worth more than a kingdom.
—WILLIAM BENNETT

What you see is mainly what you look for.
—ANONYMOUS

mirror—a large piece of reflective glass prominently displayed in the hall-way downstairs—offered a wavy, image-altering reflection of your face and form, much like a mirror in an amusement park. Given this experience, you would naturally develop a distorted opinion of yourself until you viewed your reflected image in a flawless mirror; even then, it might be surprisingly difficult to believe that the looking glass you grew up with was not a true reflection of your actual appearance.

All of us, to a greater or lesser degree, share this experience. It is only when we see ourselves with new eyes—in the light of biblical truth, according to God's perfect love for us—that we can begin to clearly identify the false reflections of ourselves that we grew up believing.

For more than a few of us, substantial adjustment is required to bring the picture into better focus. Sadly, not all mothers have adequate family support, financial resources, emotional and physical health, practical wisdom, or spiritual strength. Some feel insecure about their mothering abilities and become overwhelmed at times with the responsibilities and demands of child rearing. Some, barely able to make ends meet, must depend on unreliable caregivers while they're away working at low-paying jobs. Others, lacking the skills or social network necessary to prevent abusive behavior, lash out with verbal or physical blows that shatter their children's self-esteem and steal their sense of security. These are the stories that break our hearts.

Those of us who were the daughters of mothers who could not provide sufficient nurture or protection know we have lost something precious. For us, it still hurts to think about the reflections we saw in the mirror of our mothers' faces. We desire to give a different legacy to our daughters.

Jamie's story, recounted to me nearly 20 years after the event described here, provides a glimpse of what this experience can look like:

> My mom was a very attractive woman, and still is. I remem-
> ber her taking great pride in her appearance and spending many
> hours at the beauty salon, having her hair colored, getting her
> nails done, undergoing leg waxing. Her sense of style in cloth-

ing and cosmetics was absolutely amazing.

For years, I was awed by my mother's appearance: I wanted to look just like her when I grew up. But when I entered high school, I promptly put on extra weight, which soon proved to be a constant point of friction between us. Calories were introduced as a discussion topic at almost every meal. Diet books were left on my bed with bookmarks highlighting the pages my mom wanted me to read. At one point, Mom—who wore size-four clothes and looked great in them—even had me weigh in with her on a daily basis.

The turning point came on the day of my junior prom. By that time, I was wearing a size twelve and weighed about 138 pounds, which for someone of my height (5'8") is not unhealthy or abnormal in any way. And yet, when the moment arrived for me to walk into the living room dressed in full evening attire, I felt HUGE. If only Mom had looked at me with love instead of barely concealed discomfort, maybe it would have seemed okay somehow.

Instead, she said only, "We were fortunate to find a dress that fits you so well, Jamie."

That was it. No praise for the result of my nine-hour effort to effect some sort of magical transformation from an awkward adolescent into a fairy-tale princess on her way to the ball. No comforting remarks about my

"I have a daughter with whom I can share hopes and dreams, and who can share her hopes and dreams with me. We have a wonderful relationship—and she's a teen!"
—SUSAN, AGE 44

The more a child becomes aware of a mother's willingness to listen, the more a mother will begin to hear.
—ANONYMOUS

The patience and the humility of the face she loved so well was a better lesson to Jo than the wisest lecture, the sharpest reproof.
—LOUISA MAY ALCOTT

own special brand of beauty. No statement made about me.

The words wounded me in ways I wouldn't recognize until many years later. I still wonder sometimes why it was so hard for my mother to give me her admiration and approval, to say the words that would have made such a big difference at that critical moment. Then I think: *The way Mom looked at me is probably the way she saw herself.*

Jamie's poignant story is a vivid example of the way the "mother mirror" works. In reality, Jamie's appearance radiated good health and eye-pleasing attractiveness. But the image that Jamie "saw" on prom night based upon her mother's reflection wasn't accurate. It was a painfully blurred impression.

My purpose in sharing Jamie's story is not to recommend that we blame our mothers for serving as imperfect mirrors in our lives. They, too, learned to see themselves through flawed human reflections. And, like us, their mothers were not the sole source of their identities.

Fathers, siblings, extended family, friends, neighbors, church groups, classmates, and schoolteachers—all supply strong feedback and not-to-be-discounted information that affects one's self-image. The culture we grow up in also plays a prominent role in shaping our opinions and attitudes about who we are. (In an era when the average American television viewer sees about 650 TV commercials each week, in a nation in which the average model or actress is thinner than 95 percent of the female population, why should it shock us when research reveals that at least five out of 10 fourth-grade girls have already started dieting?[1])

I tell Jamie's story because, perhaps more than ever before, we need encouragement to act as our daughters' advocates, protectors, and guardians. We need to be their mothers, not their judges or competitors. The reflections we show our daughters about their identities—about who they are, as opposed to who we *wish* they were—deserve to be as clear, accurate, and affirming as we can make them.

Adjusting Our Focus

The first step we can make in this direction lies in taking care of unfinished business left over from our own experiences as daughters. Recalling the ways our mothers mirrored our reflections back to us can help heal the wounds of the past so we may move with greater confidence and wisdom into the future.

For women whose mothers listened attentively and provided consistent, caring affirmation, the memories are primarily pleasant and satisfying. Their mothers' interpersonal skills provided a running "head start" that gave them a distinct advantage when adulthood arrived, allowing for a greater sense of ease and self-esteem when building new relationships on their own. These daughters also seem more likely to want to model their lives after their moms' nurturing examples.

As 27-year-old Julie described it: "My mom made herself available to me when I needed to talk. She showed me a lot of love and affection and encouraged me by making me feel like I could succeed—that I had her complete support. I think the most helpful thing that happened in our relationship was that my mother let me know she trusted me, starting very early. Because of this, I have always tried to be very honest and respect her. This actually prevented a lot of conflicts and is one of the things I appreciate most about how she raised me."

For women raised by mothers who were not actively engaged in listening to, nurturing, and verbally affirming their daughters, it can feel as if they are starting from scratch when building their

"I love my mother very much. I just don't like her. She has so much trouble communicating her feelings and handling the feelings of others. If I could just get across this one point: Feelings are facts and need to be acknowledged, not stuffed."

—ANN, AGE 23

———— ✑ ————

Dear Mamma, if you
Just could be
A tiny little girl like me,
And I your Mamma,
You would see
How nice I'd be to you.
—MRS. SYDNEY DAY

———— ✑ ————

"I've always thought that my mom couldn't understand me—especially when I was hurting or upset—so I've felt like I couldn't talk to her."
—MELISSA, AGE 20

own family relationships. Without a satisfying role model upon which to base their own mothering, it is up to these women to create their own life-patterns based upon what they learn through books, classes, church instruction, and watching other women raise their daughters. Rather than being the exception to the rule, it seems that many women today choose to learn about mothering in this way.

My friend Margaret, a pastor's wife and the mother of three teenage daughters, is an encouraging example to me of someone who is a strong, capable mom who was raised by a difficult and demanding mother. When I first met Margaret, I never guessed that she had not learned her mothering skills at home while growing up. Margaret appears to be a "natural" at mothering, plain and simple. She's the kind of mom other women appreciatively emulate on an everyday basis.

Behind the scenes, however, Margaret struggles daily to love and accept her nonnurturing mother. The realization that "Mom can't see me" remains a difficult aspect of her life.

"My mother was, and is, unable to enter my world. I would say that she is uninterested in my life, or, at best, is disinterested," confided my friend. "Our conversation is almost always on her choice of topic—almost always her life or her happenings, though she can listen to me talk about my children if it isn't for too long. Communication is very difficult because Mother doesn't 'hear' me: She loses interest in what I am saying before I finish; she always 'tops' me (her story is better, more interesting). She is almost always unable to say 'you' to me. Her central word is 'I.'"

If she had not told me about her experiences as the daughter of a high-need mother, I would have guessed that Margaret's mother was a smart, gracious, brave, tenderhearted, humorous mom like Margaret. But daughters rarely become exactly what their mothers' reflections depict.

Honestly acknowledging the past and realizing that we are powerless to change it, as Margaret has, fosters genuine understanding of our mothers and how they have affected our lives. Isn't it reassuring to realize we don't need to have affirming moms who "saw" and "heard" us while we were growing up in order to become affirming moms who see and hear our own daughters today? The imperfect reflections we saw in our mothers—and our children see in us—do not ultimately determine who we become, *"for we are God's workmanship, created in Christ Jesus to do good works, which God prepared in advance for us to do"* (Eph. 2:10, emphasis added). And our Creator's sovereign design—His purposes for our lives—cannot be destroyed or defeated.

The following exercise is designed to prompt recall of some of the varied reflections your mother revealed about you through her touch, voice, eyes, and actions. This may help you recognize the mirrored messages you chose to believe as you were growing up, so that you may begin replacing them with a more accurate picture.

Messages in the Mirror: True or False?

1. Make a list of messages your mother has given to you about yourself, then examine them carefully. A list of sample statements and actions is provided below.

2. Mark each message with a T (true) or F (false). Which ones, whether true or false, did you choose to believe? Place an X by these messages.

3. Circle any messages that you saw, heard, or felt most clearly. Were there any messages that your mother never gave you that you believed she did? Write these down.

4. Read the messages once more. Copy the ones

There are no perfect mother-daughter relationships. We will not—and, in fact, cannot—love our mothers or our daughters without making mistakes.

— ❧ —

Keep your feet on a steady path, so that the limping foot does not collapse but recovers strength.
—HEBREWS 12:13,
J. B. PHILLIPS

— ❧ —

Children learn early in life that life is either a gift to be enjoyed or a burden to be borne.
—JOHN BOWLBY

— ❧ —

It is essential to practise the walk of the feet in the light of the vision.
—OSWALD CHAMBERS

you want to keep on a separate piece of paper. Cross out the messages that were false or harmful, replacing them with true and accurate statements on the second sheet of paper. Tuck your new list in your Bible or another safe place for future reference.

Sample Statements

I love you.	You're stupid.
Why don't you ever change?	You're the sweetest girl I know.
I'm very proud of you.	Do it now, or I'll let you have it!
I can see that you feel bad about that.	Hurry up, slowpoke.
What a klutz you are!	You're beautiful, dear.
You're a terrific daughter.	I appreciate you.
Take your time. I'm listening.	I like hugging you.
I'm happy you're here.	If at first you don't succeed, try again.
Cleanliness is next to godliness.	Are you sure you want to eat that?
I like the way you look.	Get away from me.
I wish you hadn't been born.	I'm proud of the way you did that today.
Be happy.	What was your favorite thing today?

She is our brainy one.

You do well, considering you're so . . .

I like being with you.

I need you.

Shut up, stupid.

You are a talented singer.

You are a spoiled brat.

Thank you for your help.

She's a big girl for her age.

I can't believe you just did/said that.

Why can't you be like your sister?

I accept your apology. I forgive you.

It's okay to try again. I'm watching.

I'm so glad you shared that with me.

If it weren't for you, I'd be happier.

Get out of my way.

I'll be here if you need my help.

How are you?

It's sinful to boast like that.

I can't believe how much you're like me.

Since we live by the Spirit, let us keep in step with the Spirit.
—*GALATIANS 5:25*

———— ❧ ————

"In both my relationships, with my mother and my daughter, it's difficult to deal with traits in myself that I see mirrored in them. Sometimes I don't even realize that it is not the situation that's stressful, but the behavioral traits I don't like that are causing the stress."
—*VONDA, AGE 38*

———— ❧ ————

Before a child can say kindness, *he can understand the forgiving smile on his mother's face; before he can spell* God, *he can sense his mother's anxiety dissipate as she talks to Someone he cannot even see.*
—*JILL BRISCOE*

You're ugly.

Don't do this . . .
do this instead.

You look ridiculous in
that dress.

Can we talk later? I'm busy.

I know you'll be careful.

You're selfish.

Thanks for cooperating
with me.

I wish you were a boy.

I am thankful you were born.

You'll never learn to do
that right!

Thank you for being *you*.

Excellent work!

You think well, for a girl.

I wish someone else were
your mother.

Nice job, honey!

I like you.

I trust you.

You are a bad girl.

I like you when you take
care of me.

You make superb drawings.

I enjoy our time together
very much.

You're a joy!

Sample Actions

Hugging	Kissing	Stroking
Cuddling	Patting	Holding hands
Shoving	Hitting	Ignoring
Warm eye contact	Smiling	Nodding
Turning away	Glaring	Yelling

Addressing child by name

Listening

Reinforcing boundaries

Laughing together

Spending time together

Doing things together

Love Lessons

Through Christ, we can discover our true identities as we submit our lives to Him and cast our cares upon our King. He gives us peace for our hearts and heals the wounds we experienced in flawed family relationships. We cannot change the past and cannot change the people in it. *No matter how much we wish things could be different, the void in our lives that we may feel in relationship to our mothers—and daughters—can be filled only by God.*

When I became a Christian 26 years ago, one of the leading factors in my decision to seek God's help and surrender my life to Christ was my relationship with my mother. Years of conflict between us had produced a gaping wound in my heart that nothing could touch. Painful memories desperately needed healing. I felt helpless to undo the harm that my chronically ill mother's emotional needs had caused in my life. Nor could I release myself from the guilt I suffered about how I had treated her during my adolescence in response to her abusive behavior.

"Isn't it difficult to see our own flaws in our daughters? What a true mess it would be without God's grace to protect them and cover the mistakes we make!"
—PENNY, AGE 44

— ✍ —

Wisdom is at home in a discerning mind.
—PROVERBS 14:33A, NEB

— ✍ —

The best portion of a Good man's life,
His little, nameless,
Unremembered acts
Of kindness and love.
—WILLIAM WORDSWORTH

— ✍ —

The past must be abandoned to God's mercy, the present to our fidelity, the future to divine providence.
—FRANCIS DE SALES

Kneeling beside my bed on a bright, snow-covered January afternoon, I told God I believed He was there, and I wanted to know the best way to follow Him. How could I know and understand Him better? In particular, I asked God to help me love the people to whom I was closest.

"Nothing I've been doing—the yoga classes, breathing methods, macrobiotic diets, meditation, positive thinking—has significantly improved my ability to care for people," I prayed, "including my mother."

As an 18-year-old emerging from a troubled adolescence, I knew that I didn't have the ability to forgive Mom for the pain she had inflicted earlier in my life. I was hurting too badly. The demeaning and destructive words we had said to one another at different times had gone too deep. I needed God's cleansing forgiveness and healing help.

Within weeks, I started attending an informal Bible study with a fellow student on the campus of Wayne State University, and soon I began following Christ. Although I would like to be able to tell you that my relationship with my mom was instantly healed upon my conversion to Christianity, I can't. I am still learning about what it means to understand, accept, and love her. But I have learned that as my capacity to trust God to fill the void and soothe the ache enlarges, as I let go of my expectations and give up my attempts to control the course of our relationship, as I view Mom's gifts and personality with new eyes from a changed perspective, I find my love for her grows.

For example, shortly after Christmas last year, Mom and I were standing in the kitchen discussing our plans for the day when I felt an unexpected surge of tenderness toward her. I reached out to give her a big hug, and as my hands touched her back, I detected the sharp curvature in her spine she had so often talked about. A wave of compassion temporarily knocked out every one of the defenses I had formed over the past 40 years to shield myself from her pain. Without warning, I felt her chronic disability in a way that had been previously inaccessible to my mind and heart.

Mom's back injury had taken place six years before my birth. I have never known her as a fully functioning, pain-free woman. The burden of my mother's struggle to cope with the aftermath of her life-changing accident was a load our family shared every day. At some point, when things got really rough between us, I stopped hearing her too-familiar complaints and turned off my sensitivity toward her condition. Yet there I was, many years later, feeling the hurt in a healthy way for the first time, hugging Mom's spine through her terry-cloth robe, experiencing a totally out-of-the-blue explosion of God's grace that only the Holy Spirit could have produced.

A host of moments such as this one have been given to my mother and me over the course of our lives in Christ. Lately, they seem to be happening with greater frequency. Prayer, counseling, forgiveness, reading books that provide insight, listening to other women's stories, and growing older have substantially assisted the mending process. But, most of all, I credit the healing of our relationship to God.

Beyond Perfection

There are no perfect mother-daughter relationships. We will not—and, in fact, cannot—love our mothers or our daughters without making mistakes. Though some mother-daughter pairs approach our ideal of what such a shared bond might be, perfection in human relationships is not possible this side of heaven.

So, why do we believe that it is? Maybe part of the reason we cling to this false hope is because once we

Concrete reasons for loving another human being not only need to be expressed to that person, but will also help the person who is doing the verbalizing. . . . Love will grow as reasons for love are discovered, thought about, dwelt upon in the mind, expressed verbally, and remembered.
—*EDITH SCHAEFFER*

———— ✍ ————

A labor of love is never lost in heaven's eyes.
—*ANONYMOUS*

———— ✍ ————

The eyes of the world see no further than this life, as mine see no further than this wall when the church door is shut. The eyes of the Christian see deeply into Eternity.
—*JOHN VIANNEY*

admit to ourselves that perfection is not possible, we must open our eyes and face things as they actually are. Then what happens?

What can happen is that we can learn to depend upon God's strength as He helps us acknowledge and forgive one another's faults, fears, and failings. We can work at adjusting the ideal to fit the real, according to what the Bible teaches us about living in a world where death, disease, and sin affect every family. We can look at our daughters and recognize who they are, instead of who we would like them to be, maybe for the first time. We can remind ourselves that one of the greatest gifts we can give to our daughters is a mirror where they can find love colorfully and truthfully reflected. Finally, we can nurture and protect our daughters' one-of-a-kind combination of temperament, talent, and personality by accurately appraising their distinctive blend of strengths and weaknesses.

Making identity diagrams of my two daughters' unique traits and characteristics has been a valuable resource in enabling me to establish clear mental portraits of Joanna and Katherine. It has been an especially effective tool during stressful moments when my tendency toward anxious criticism pulls me inward and diminishes my ability to see my daughters accurately. It also has been helpful in reminding me of their striking individuality. Recalling these diagrams and asking God for patience and understanding makes me more inclined to stick to a steady course of mothering.

Identity Diagram

An *identity diagram* is a basic chart of a person's one-of-a-kind qualities and characteristics. It is a practical tool that can help us affirm and honor our daughters by reminding us to recognize our children's lovable uniqueness at critical moments—the times when we're particularly vulnerable to saying and doing the things we may regret later.

When making your daughter's chart (space for this exercise is provided at the end of this chapter), you may wish to use the following six categories, as well as any others that are helpful to you. You may also want to ask for your daughter's assistance before making the diagram—by having her fill out a list of personal favorites, by conducting an informal mother-daughter interview, or by simply asking about any areas of her life into which you want to gain insight.

1. *Present-at-birth characteristics*—the attributes your daughter has in common with all people.
2. *Personality and temperament*—your daughter's unique, built-in emotional attributes, intellectual qualities, and way of relating to others.
3. *Gifts and talents*—the God-given skills, aptitudes, and abilities your daughter possesses.
4. *Passions and preferences*—any likes and dislikes, hobbies and interests, and tastes and inclinations your daughter has acquired since childhood.
5. *Beliefs and values*—how your daughter views and relates to God and the world, as well as everyone and everything in it.
6. *Goals and aspirations*—the wide-ranging assortment of hopes and dreams that are inspiring your daughter's future outlook.

Here is a sample diagram that you may use as a guide in developing your daughter's descriptive portrait:

1. *Present-at-birth characteristics:* Worthy of love; valued creation; unique personality; protected by angels; known by Christ; person in possession of eternal soul; child of God.
2. *Personality and temperament:* Outgoing, talkative, thoughtful, serious, compassionate, imaginative, dramatic, self-critical, dreamer.

The maturity of Christian experience cannot be reached in a moment, but is the result of the work of God's Holy Spirit, who, by His energizing and transforming power, causes us to grow up into Christ in all things.
—HANNAH WHITALL
SMITH

—— ✐ ——

The one thing for which we have been created is the doing of the will of God.
—JAMES S. STEWART

—— ✐ ——

We often pray for purity, unselfishness, for the highest qualities of character, and forget that these things cannot be given, but must be earned.
—LYMAN ABBOTT

3. *Gifts and talents:* Merciful, tenderhearted, spiritually sensitive, humorous, loyal, artistic, musical, problem-solver, creative thinker, leader.

4. *Passions and preferences:* Calligraphy, campfires, cats, Christmas, basketball, handwritten letters, pizza, Snickers, tuna fish sandwiches, Dr Pepper, vintage clothes, *The Sound of Music,* lavender soap, choral groups, Emily Dickinson's poems, Fourth of July fireworks, pottery making, fresh raspberries, birthday parties, Psalm 91, *A Christmas Carol,* comical postcards, peppermint tea, fishing at grandparents' cabin, the color blue, loving Jesus.

5. *Beliefs and values:* "God rules"; the Golden Rule ("Do unto others as you would have them do unto you"); the Ten Commandments; get a good education; help the poor; share the gospel; attend church; spend time outdoors; read the Bible; reach for your goals; be creative; be kind to animals; "Jesus lives"; human life is precious; all people are created equal; people are more important than things; don't tell on your friends; love God; love your family; love your enemies; guard your heart; God answers prayer.

6. *Goals and aspirations:* Attend college; teach English as a second language in a foreign country; travel; be a faithful friend; play in a women's basketball league; stay close to God; minister through music; get married; start a family; promote personal health; visit Switzerland with husband; write a book of poetry; aim for heaven.

"The love of God is not mere sentimentality; it is the most practical thing for the saint to love as God loves. The springs of love are in God, not in us," observed Scottish evangelist Oswald Chambers.[2] By viewing our daughters from the Creator's perspective—and relying upon His grace to renew our vision day by day—we can mirror their special qualities back to them as the advocates, protectors, and guardians we are called to be.

Your Daughter's Identity Diagram: What Do You See in Her?

1. *Present-at-birth characteristics:*

2. *Personality and temperament:*

3. *Gifts and talents:*

4. *Passions and preferences:*

5. *Beliefs and values:*

6. *Goals and aspirations:*

Identity Diagram Worksheet

As you prepare to make your daughter's identity diagram, you may wish to use this section as a guide in becoming better acquainted with her current passions, preferences, values, beliefs, aspirations, and goals. Simply ask her to fill out a worksheet similar to the one below, or, if you prefer, conduct a live interview, discussing her replies about each area as you go along.

Favorite friends:	Favorite teacher:
Favorite pet:	Favorite animal:
Favorite relatives:	Favorite celebrities:
Favorite authors:	Favorite musicians:
Favorite movies:	Favorite books:
Favorite magazines:	Favorite TV shows:
Favorite sayings:	Favorite Bible quotes:
Favorite poems:	Favorite songs:
Favorite fragrance:	Favorite flower:
Favorite color:	Favorite clothes:
Favorite foods:	Favorite beverages:
Favorite family traditions:	Favorite vacation spot:
Favorite way to relax:	Favorite sports:
Favorite memory:	Favorite gifts:

Favorite birthday party: Favorite photos:

Favorite hobbies: Favorite form of
                                    transportation:

Favorite foreign country: Favorite city:

Favorite place to unwind: Favorite form of
                                    recreation:

I believe God is . . .

The people, places, things, and ideas I most value are . . .

In the future, I hope to be able to . . .

When I grow up, I want to be / My career choice at this point is . . .

I would describe myself as . . .

Recovering Our Losses

Forgiving is the only way to heal the wounds of a past we cannot change and cannot forget. Forgiving changes a bitter memory into a grateful memory, a cowardly memory into a courageous memory, an enslaved memory into a free memory. Forgiving restores a self-respect that someone killed. And, more than anything else, forgiving gives birth to hope for the future after our past illusions have been shattered.

—*Lewis B. Smedes*

Chapter Four

————— ❧ —————

No one could have guessed the truth about Michelle's family background, given the caring devotion she displayed toward her three young daughters. Many people viewed Michelle as an inspiring model of motherhood—tutoring her children, feeding the girls nutritious meals, teaching Sunday school class every week, leading a weekly Bible study group for young mothers. What they didn't see was Michelle's private struggle to forgive and forget the daily chaos of growing up in a family that had been deeply affected by her mother's addiction to alcohol.

Michelle's perfectionism in mothering seemed a suitable response, given what she believed a mother *should* be. For many years, it appeared that she was on the right track as she created the kind of home environment she had longed for during her own childhood. But after Michelle had been a mother for about 12 years, she developed irritable bowel syndrome and a number of other chronic health problems. A two-year bout with borderline depression followed.

About the time her oldest daughter, Maribeth, turned 15 years old, Michelle's emotional state worsened. After taking the girls to school in the morning, she routinely went back to bed for several hours every day, finding it nearly impossible to get up before noon. By nine o'clock at night, unrelenting exhaustion once again made sleep irresistible. Though Michelle remained outwardly calm and considerate, she frequently experienced self-destructive thoughts, sometimes even imagining her own death as a means of escaping her oppressive inner anguish.

Surprisingly, not even her husband, Warren, recognized the symptoms. Believing that Michelle's fatigue resulted from a temporary overload of family responsibilities, he encouraged his wife to get more rest, suggested she take additional vitamins, and voluntarily performed extra household tasks. Michelle's friends also underestimated the extent of her private crisis. Because their normally buoyant companion exhibited no external signs of distress, they assumed she was the same person she had always been: an extremely capable and loving Christian woman, wife, and mother. On the inside, however, Michelle felt incompetent, isolated, unlovable—and numb.

The turning point came when Warren lost his job due to budget cutbacks, forcing the family of five to leave their comfortable home in a small southeastern town. After relocating to a fast-paced metropolitan area in the Northwest, Michelle hunted for a church home, feeling relieved that she didn't have to put up a front any longer. Why should she? The parishioners at Saint Matthew's, the family's freshly chosen congregation, had no inkling of Michelle's aptitudes and abilities. And so she offered nothing, content to remain out of the spotlight, gratefully trading her center-stage role in South Carolina for the anonymity of a back-corner pew in the heart of downtown Seattle.

The loneliness—and lack of close friends' expectations—brought an unexpected blessing: Michelle stopped pretending. Realizing that her coping skills couldn't shield her family from the devastating effects of her depression, Michelle phoned for help. Her new pastor pointed the way out of the wilderness.

"Once we moved away from our well-established support group, I couldn't fool myself about my fatigue anymore. When I heard that our new church sponsored a counseling and support group program, I set up an appointment immediately."

Recalling how long it took her to seek help, Michelle shook her head and smiled. "You know, up until that year we moved to Washington, I sincerely believed I could study—or pray—my way out of every single seemingly insurmountable situation. Then God taught me to trust Him more deeply.

"Having to face the pain and conflict of my own adolescence seemed so unfair," Michelle admitted. "More than anything, I wanted to believe that I was beyond all of that, that as a grown woman, I could unconditionally love and support my own children very well, thank you. *I wanted to be the one in control instead of giving God control of my life and my family.* But to get beyond the pain of my past, I needed to face it with concentrated prayer and skilled Christian guidance, from an adult's vantage point instead of a child's."

In retrospect, Michelle said, the underlying causes of her depression were clear. "When the girls were young, I really excelled at being the kind of mother I'd always wanted. Mothering my daughters brought me the opportunity, although in a round-about way, to 're-mother' myself. But Maribeth's

---

If you are a Christian, your final environment is a world whose creator forgives, accepts, and loves you in all your uniqueness.
—DICK KEYES

——— ✍ ———

The LORD your God is with you, he is mighty to save. He will take great delight in you, he will quiet you with his love, he will rejoice over you with singing.
—ZEPHANIAH 3:17

——— ✍ ———

Guilt and shame are not friends of grace that prompt inner healing.
—CHUCK SWINDOLL

——— ✍ ———

With the help of God, you can forgive those who have hurt you, and thereby you will become a better mother to your children.
—BRENDA HUNTER

entrance into full-fledged puberty—the time when every mom must accept a less central, more limited role in her daughter's life—provoked my emotional shutdown. It was as if I had been abandoned by my own mother all over again."

Today, Michelle is increasingly able to accept her three daughters' emerging independence and contrasting personalities with honesty, humor, and grace. Viewing motherhood as a dynamic progression of distinctly different growth stages—through her daughters' infancy, early childhood, preadolescence, teenage years, and beyond—she is gaining a fresh appreciation for her God-given gifts while investing her talents in new ways as a part-time university librarian and small-group coleader at her church.

With an ever-widening sphere of ministry opening up before her, Michelle thanks God for enabling her to honestly experience a colorful range of emotions without false guilt. Many days, she faces the future with joy.

The last time I spoke to her, she told me:

> If we hadn't moved, how long would I have been able to fool everyone, including myself? What if I had simply stayed numb throughout Maribeth's high school years and never discovered the true cause of my inner paralysis, continuing to act as if nothing were wrong? How could I have assumed for so long that I had completely forgiven my mother after I became a Christian? That I didn't bitterly resent my dad for not protecting me from my mom's abuse? Or that I could change the legacy by doing things "right" with my children, without working through and praying over the far-reaching impact of my own family upbringing?
>
> My daughters gave me a valuable gift: a second chance to work things through with my mother. As a result, I feel a new tenderness toward her. I've gained a deeper understanding of why she acted the way she did when I became a teenager. Rather than feeling angry or afraid, I'm more sympathetic. I also recognize my limitations in our relationship more clearly: I can't be the perfect, all-fulfilling daughter any more than she can be my ideal

of what a mother should be. Making peace with Mom is making me a healthier mother *and* daughter.

Giving Up Our Illusions

Growing into adulthood and raising a daughter bring us face to face with our mothers. As we gradually move from a state of complete dependence to the safe distance of interdependence, we may find ourselves pushing toward total *independence* from our mothers, as Michelle did. But, sooner or later, we discover a profound truth: No matter how far we go, our mothers go with us.

Our self-acceptance is intricately interwoven with our ability to make peace with our mothers. Blaming our mothers cannot heal the wounds. Cutting ourselves away from our family roots is not a cure.

Not surprisingly, many women do this anyway. Think for a moment about the countless times you have heard a friend say something similar to one of these statements:

- "Mom and I are totally different. I really can't relate to her."

- "I understand that my mother came from a difficult family. But she should have done more to undo some of the damage. Why should I be the one to reach out to her after the way she's treated me?"

- "I'm glad that my mom and I live 2,000 miles apart. Seeing her once or twice per year is about all I can handle."

Make me a captive, Lord,
And then I shall be free;
Force me to render up
my sword,
And I shall conqueror be.
I sink in life's alarms
When by myself I stand;
Imprison me within
Thine arms,
And strong shall be my
hand.
—GEORGE MATHESON

———— ✍ ————

"I want to stop feeling angry in my heart toward my mother. I hope I never hurt my children the way she has hurt me."
—SUSAN, AGE 44

———— ✍ ————

Lord, when doubts fill my mind, when my heart is in turmoil, quiet me and give me renewed hope and cheer.
—PSALM 94:19, TLB

———— ✍ ————

A wounded spirit who can bear?
—PROVERBS 18:14B, KJV

- "When it comes to being around my parents, I prefer spending time with my dad. We always got along better than my mom and I did."

- "Mother and I get along well, considering I can hardly stand her sometimes. I listen to what she has to say, but it doesn't have much of an effect on me."

- "I wish Mom and I were closer. But I've come to accept that this will never happen, given who we are."

- "My mother is such a child. I feel like a mature adult compared with her."

When we were young children, we believed in an idealized version of our mothers as a necessary means of securing our emotional stability. Living in a state of complete dependence upon maternal comfort and care, we overlooked our moms' weaknesses for the most part, preferring instead to focus on their strengths. Believing Mom was good helped us to feel good about ourselves. But somewhere along the line, we began to see our mothers more objectively. As we grew up, we discovered that at least a few of our earlier beliefs were actually illusions.

This transition may happen quite smoothly or, as in cases like Michelle's, it may get stuck, bogged down in the resentment or bitterness that follows the loss of our idealized versions of our mothers. Coming to terms with this loss and mending from the pain, with God's help, allows us to more completely enter adulthood. It frees us to fully face our feelings of grief and disappointment, enabling us to forgive. It allows us to lay down the heavy weight of the leftover baggage we're carrying and may lead to genuine family reconciliation—including the establishment of a mutually satisfying, mature friendship between mother and daughter.

At this point, you may be considering putting this book down and never picking it up again. You may be thinking that you will never have the kind of mutually satisfying, mature friendship you would like to have with your mother because she is _____ (fill in the blank). Perhaps your mom, like Michelle's, is suffering under the weight of personal addiction to alcohol, food, dieting, relationships, spending money, exercise, work, or self-beautification. Maybe she has a personality disorder or other form of mental illness that makes the formation of healthy family bonds seem an insurmountable challenge. She might be so busy with her own life—with a new job, new husband, new demands—that you feel she has no time for you. Or your mother may have died before you could make peace with her, precluding reconciliation during your lifetime.

If you are struggling with one of these, or any other, painful realities concerning your relationship with your mother, I don't blame you for feeling discouraged, grief-stricken, cynical, or angry. My question to you is simply: *Where do you want to go from here?* If you are satisfied with the way things are, why attempt to change anything? But if you desire to find peace, and perhaps a certain measure of reconciliation, in your relationship with your mother, it will mean honestly facing your feelings toward her and asking God to help you let go of the hurt. Not all at once. Not right this minute. Not today, or even tomorrow, but over the coming days, months, and years.

As a step in this direction, you may want to consider keeping a journal about your relationship with your mom. Write down whatever thoughts, memories, feelings, and reflections come to mind.

The art of being wise is the art of knowing what to overlook.
—WILLIAM JAMES

— ❧ —

Our self-acceptance is intricately interwoven with our ability to make peace with our mothers.

— ❧ —

Nobody who has not been in the interior of a family can say what the difficulties of any individual of that family may be.
—JANE AUSTEN

— ❧ —

Search me, O God, and know my heart; test me and know my anxious thoughts. See if there is any offensive way in me, and lead me in the way everlasting.
—PSALM 139:23–24

— ❧ —

We win by tenderness; we conquer by forgiveness.
—FREDERICK WILLIAM ROBERTSON

When you are ready, make a list of hurts and resentments you have toward your mother. Be specific. No one but the Lord need ever know what you have written. And never show the list to your mother, no matter how angry you may feel at times. Your reason for keeping this journal is, after all, aimed at mending your relationship and promoting healing for your wounds. Confessing difficult feelings, painful memories, and lingering resentments to God brings them out of the darkness of your past into the light of Jesus' redemptive presence (1 John 1:5–9). It does not guarantee that your mother will become the mom you've always wanted, or that she will change her behavior, or even that reconciliation is possible this side of heaven. But *you* will be changed, and that is all you are responsible for.

As Christ's lordship enlarges to cover every area of your life, you will find the peace, joy, and freedom He promises to His followers. It's guaranteed. At some point, you may also want to share what you are learning with your husband, sister, or trusted friend. If you need advice in addition to the solace of this type of supportive listening, seek confidential assistance from a competent Christ-centered counselor. Get the help and the prayer you need to move beyond the past and be released from the tight grip of emotional pain, fear, grief, or discouragement you are experiencing.

Moving from the Ideal to the Real

As destructive generational patterns are deliberately examined, prayed over, and amended, the false notions of motherhood we have chosen to believe in—that mothers can be perfect if they just try hard enough, that good mothers never get angry, and that the way children behave is direct proof of their mothers' level of competence—are given up in favor of an honest appraisal and acceptance of who mothers actually are: fallible women who make mistakes. Blame no longer belongs in the picture.

Then an interesting thing happens: We stop feeling compelled to live up to the impossible dream ourselves. We know, once and for all, that we are not destined to repeat our mothers' mistakes. And we teach our daughters as they are growing up that we are real human beings instead of ideal models of perfection.

I remember my friend Judy describing her struggle with postpartum depression after the births of her two daughters and the ongoing feelings of inadequacy that followed.

"Having children was so different from what I expected," she shared. "It turned out that my ideas about motherhood had little to do with reality and much to do with the Laura Ingalls Wilder books I grew up reading. When things got tough in my own family, *The Little House on the Prairie* became my fantasy of an ideal family. Later, I couldn't understand why real life couldn't be the same as it was in those wonderful stories."

I can identify with Judy's frustration. In my own life, I've tried to make the ideal fit the real on many occasions. Unrealistic pictures of motherhood (that mothers tenderly answer all irksome inquiries, never lose their tempers, cope with every life crisis calmly, always maintain their self-control, and always guide their children with a firm yet gentle hand) are attractive ideals in the face of harsh daily realities that require difficult solutions. Who, after reading *Little Women*, doesn't aspire to be like Jo's Marmee, a mother who sets an inspiring example of womanhood

Our emotions belong to us, and are suffered and enjoyed by us, but they are not ourselves; and if God is to take possession of us, it must be into this central will or personality that he enters.
—HANNAH WHITALL SMITH

———— ❧ ————

If the injured one could read your heart, you may be sure he would understand and pardon.
—ROBERT LOUIS STEVENSON

———— ❧ ————

"As a young adult, I felt very rejected because of my mother's lack of interest in me. But as I have grown older—and now understand her life better—I have come to terms with this. I have forgiven and accepted her and have gone on to receive healing."
—LINDA, AGE 38

by providing steady, sage advice, kind affirmation, loving embraces, and tender bedside nursing care for her daughters—behaviors we would all do well to emulate. And yet, is it really realistic that Marmee also manages not to complain, even once, in spite of terrible family hardships, and she never embarrasses herself by bursting out in anger or tears at an awkward moment? Impossible feats for any real woman! Watching Clair Huxtable on syndicated reruns of *The Cosby Show*, why *wouldn't* we want always to be smart, attractive, gracious, elegant, witty, well-dressed, and super-competent, too? And that isn't all bad. I believe God calls us to pursue excellence for His glory in every area of our lives—to aim to do our best with the talents, resources, time, skills, and tools He gives us. It's when we make the mistake of categorizing mothers as either saints or sinners that we get into trouble. Because, like it or not, our humanity humbles us. We sometimes say or do the things we do not want to say or do. Like the apostle Paul, we find ourselves frequently frustrated by our flesh, because we are not—and cannot ever be—perfect this side of heaven.

This is good news. We are not designed to depend on human fantasies and ideals, but on God alone, as our sole source of life, hope, strength, and vision. Substitutes, no matter who or what they are, will never satisfy us. We are designed to hunger after the fruits of the Holy Spirit instead (Gal. 5:22–23):

- Love
- Joy
- Peace
- Patience
- Kindness
- Goodness
- Faithfulness
- Gentleness
- Self-control

When we feel discouraged, we can choose to turn to God for strength and peace. When we are in turmoil, we can ask Him to comfort us and remind us of His grace. When we find our attempts to reach our false ideals becoming frustrated by our humanity, we can single-mindedly seek the Holy Spirit's satisfying sustenance. We can stop living according to conditioned childhood responses and unrealistic mothering ideals as we forgive our mothers—and increasingly learn to accept the freedom Christ offers us day by day through His cleansing forgiveness and unconditional love.

Peace and union are the most necessary of all things for men who live in common, and nothing serves so well to establish and maintain them as the forbearing charity whereby we put up with one another's defects.
—ROBERT BELLARMINE

Don't let the world around you squeeze you into its mold, but let God re-make you so that your whole attitude of mind is changed. Thus you will prove in practice that the will of God is good, acceptable to him and perfect.
—ROMANS 12:2,
J. B. PHILLIPS

My Mother's Biography

Write a biography of your mother—her life story. Many women find this to be a valuable exercise that gives them a healing perspective not only of their mothers' lives, but of their own lives and their daughters' lives as well.

Looking into your mother's history may lead you down a road of discovery that will surprise you. As you consider your mother's background and experiences—the little girl she once was, as well as the woman she eventually became—your compassion for her is likely to deepen, *even as you recognize the pain she may have caused you.*

The biography can be anything from a brief sketch to a full-blown account. Interviews, personal accounts of childhood experiences, scrapbooks, family photo albums, old letters, and a list of accomplishments are some of the sources you may find especially helpful. The more complete and accurate your research is, the greater will be the depth of your final portrait.

Practicing Patience Through Prayer

Be not angry that you cannot make others as you wish them to be, since you cannot make yourself as you wish to be. . . . First keep the peace within yourself, then you can also bring peace to others.

—Thomas à Kempis

Chapter Five

───── ❧ ─────

$\mathcal{P}$hyllis was talking on the phone, putting away the groceries, checking her calendar, unloading the dishwasher, *and* brushing her daughter's hair, when it happened.

"Ouch!" shrieked six-year-old Shannon. "You're hurting me, Mom!"

In an instant, before she had even thought about it, Phyllis blurted out a word she hadn't used since college. Where had *that* come from?

"I can't believe I just said that, Shannon," Phyllis said immediately, with more than a little chagrin. "Will you forgive me? That's a very ugly word, and it was wrong for me to say it."

"What does it mean?" asked Shannon.

If only I had said something else! thought Phyllis as she stalled for time. *What am I supposed to say now? Ask your father? I'll explain it to you when you're older? Let's forget about it and pretend Mom never said such a thing?*

If only I had . . . It's a phrase most mothers are quite familiar with. When stress builds and hormones flash, emotional temperatures can quickly rise to the point of combustion. Cooling down at such moments is one of the primary challenges we confront regularly as Christians—and as mothers.

Compounding this task is the complexity of women's roles and routines today. We lead dynamic, busy lives that require juggling multiple schedules with our child-rearing responsibilities, marital ministrations, and personal commitments. Church ministry, community service, continuing education, and other outside activities add to the list. And, unlike many of our mothers, many of us work in full- or part-time jobs outside the home. We are as likely to be running in a regional marathon, leading a weekly Bible study, or conducting a board meeting as we are to be teaching home-school classes or driving our daughters to soccer practice. By and large, we have higher incomes, bigger bills, greater mobility, more health and beauty expectations, and a wider variety of lifestyle options than our parents had.

Is it any wonder we run out of energy and inspiration now and then?

Sign of the Times

In 1970, a poll of nearly 1,000 women found that a remarkable 52 percent of its respondents said that for them the most enjoyable aspect of being a woman was *motherhood.* In second place, at 22 percent, was *being a wife. Personal rights and freedom* came in third, at 14 percent, and, in last place, *career,* at 9 percent. A nearly identical poll conducted in 1983 pointed to the influential impact of changing cultural values concerning marriage and family life. The results? *Personal rights and freedom* jumped in popularity, from 14 to 32 percent, assuming the top position as "most enjoyable." *Career* and *motherhood* tied for second. In the later poll, 25 percent of the respondents said their careers brought them the most satisfaction, nearly three times as many as in 1970.

The total for *motherhood* had been cut in half. More significantly, the least important aspect of being a woman according to the later poll's participants was *being a wife*, which came in a distant last. Down from second place (22 percent) in the first survey, the figure for the 1983 report dipped to 6 percent—an alarming three-quarters reduction.[1] *These attitude shifts appear to represent one of the most revolutionary changes in women's ideas of marriage and family life that have ever taken place in world history.*

Given the scope of recent trends, it shouldn't surprise us that women today are at risk for developing depression, eating disorders, marriage problems, substance abuse, debting addiction (habitual overspending), digestive difficulties, and chronic reproductive health concerns. Over the past several decades, women have paid a high price for trying to "do it all," all at once. If the same poll were conducted today, would it show yet another series of remarkable changes? Is *personal rights and freedom* again lower on the priority list, with *motherhood* valued above *career* as a source of life satisfaction, and *marriage* ranking somewhere near the top? Or are we still struggling to cope with the spiritual legacy left over from three decades' worth of seismic cultural upheaval?

I do not know the answers to these questions. But I do know this: By choosing not to have it all, increasing numbers of women have realized that the investment mothers make in their children's lives is worth

Nothing else will ever make you as happy or as sad, as proud or as tired, as motherhood.
—ELIA PARSONS

———— ✍ ————

This is the one I esteem: he who is humble and contrite in spirit, and trembles at my word.
—ISAIAH 66:2B

———— ✍ ————

The virtues of mothers shall be visited upon their children.
—CHARLES DICKENS

———— ✍ ————

Beware of despairing about yourself: you are commanded to put your trust in God, and not in yourself.
—SAINT AUGUSTINE

———— ✍ ————

"My children know when all is well with my soul—and when it's not!"
—PENNY, AGE 44

the cost. We are pleased and proud to accept the privilege of becoming character trainers, identity shapers, and spiritual mentors. What's more, what other line of work pays the same amount of eternal dividends?

A Starting Point

Though the daily details of our lives may differ significantly from our predecessors in previous eras, the delights and demands of motherhood remain essentially the same. Our calling comes in the moments when we are quiet enough to hear it, and it is confirmed day by day as we learn it by heart through each new season. Now that I have a granddaughter, and have seen my oldest child become a mother, I know a kind of mothering that is making my vocation more splendid still. The calling that irresistibly beckoned me 25 years ago continues, clear and resonant, though the timbre has become deeper and richer. And I expect to keep listening for years to come. Having said these things, however, there's something I would like to add.

Few mothers receive more than minimal help from people outside their immediate families. That's a precarious position for women with so many responsibilities. Thankfully, the majority of us manage to do extraordinarily well, given the current scope and status of our role—but I have yet to meet a mom who doesn't feel overwhelmed sometimes. Even the best of us have bad days.

To be perfectly honest, being a mom has brought me to the end of myself, not once, not twice, but *countless* times. At times, I have felt tremendous pressure from friends and family, my own idealistic standards and social expectations, popular parenting experts, and supermom stereotypes found in classic literature to fulfill my multiple roles with grace, genius, calm, creativity, skill, and self-control. Like you, I've felt the strain. I've angrily screamed into my pillow so no one could hear me, daydreamed about taking an extended vacation—by myself—in an exotic location, collapsed in frustration over ridiculously small things, and wept gallons of tears. And these are only the things I'm willing to tell you about.

Please believe me when I say: *My patience ran out a long time ago!* (Sometime in the seventies, I think.) On my own, I don't have what it takes to complete my calling. My "flesh" lacks the humility and kindness, the joy and vision, and the strength and courage that capable mothering requires. Admitting this to myself took years. Accepting it inside my heart took longer.

When my youngest daughter was five years old, I remember asking her, "Do you know what *patience* means?" The question was not merely an educational exercise: I had become a bit exasperated, to say the least, over Katy's continued interruptions while I studied for a final exam. Her answer stopped me in my tracks, capturing my attention.

"Mom, don't you know what *patience* means?" the curly-haired kindergartner said with a sigh. "It means BE QUIET AND WAIT."

Katy was right. Patience *does* mean "be quiet and wait." "In repentance and rest is your salvation, in quietness and trust is your strength," the prophet Isaiah told us (Isa. 30:15). These are radical, life-changing words—a promise for help and holy intervention in the midst of our hectic, high-stress lives. Where we are lacking, God gives us His pledge that He will unfailingly supply our needs. Prayer is the starting point that opens the door to God and letting Him work in His time. As we look to Him and honestly admit, "I can't do this, Lord!" He stretches out His hands and provides the promise of peace: "Come to me, all you who are weary and burdened, and I will give you rest. Take my yoke upon you and learn from me, for I am

Worry doesn't empty tomorrow of its sorrows, it empties today of its strength.
—CORRIE TEN BOOM

——— ✍ ———

To thee I offer my outstretched hands, athirst for thee in a thirsty land. . . . Show me the way that I must take; to thee I offer all my heart.
—PSALM 143:6,8, NEB

——— ✍ ———

Listening can be a greater service than speaking.
—DIETRICH BONHOEFFER

——— ✍ ———

In the morning, prayer is the key that opens to us the treasures of God's mercies and blessings; in the evening, it is the key that shuts us up under His protection and safeguard.
—ANONYMOUS

gentle and humble in heart, and you will find rest for your souls. For my yoke is easy and my burden is light" (Matt. 11:28–30).

This is it! Here are words we can rely on, again and again, to lead us to the only everlasting source of quietness and patience. There *is* Someone who cares, who closely identifies with our feelings of loneliness, stress, and vexation. In His presence, the practice of patience becomes a team effort.

I cannot imagine what it is like to be a mother without Jesus' constant comfort and companionship. How many times have I turned to Him, full of frustration, feeling worn out, angry, or inadequate? Taking time out in His presence revives and refreshes me. Sometimes my prayers are as simple as crying out, "Help me, Lord!" or "Have mercy on me, Father." Other times they focus specifically on what is needed.

I can remember one time when my oldest daughter had stubbornly refused to take a nap. Finally, I set her down on her bed, told her to read a book, and quietly left the room. I could hear her cries of defiant protest echoing down the hallway as I ran to my bedroom, closed the door, covered my face with a pillow to muffle the noise, and screamed into the downy cushion at the top of my lungs.

At that moment, I was so tired and angry that I could have hit someone. Hard. And that someone would have probably been Joanna, had I not rushed out of the room instead.

"*Lord, I can't do this.* Joanna is driving me up the wall! I don't have the patience to be a good mom. And at this moment, I realize that I'm truly capable of doing my daughter harm. Help me, Jesus."

After resting with my eyes closed for a few moments, I looked toward the clock to see what time it was and noticed a Bible lying open on the bedside stand. Picking it up, I immediately saw that it was turned to Psalm 61. As I began to read, my tension drained out in a flood of tears, splashing on the pages as I read: "Hear my cry, O God; listen to my prayer. From the ends of the earth I call to you, I call as my heart grows faint; lead me to the rock that is higher than I. For you have been my refuge, a strong tower against the foe. I long to dwell in your tent forever and take refuge in the shelter of your wings" (Ps. 61:1–4).

Turning to God for help, we wait upon His Word and trust Him to comfort and restore us. Relying upon the Lord's grace when we would condemn ourselves for failing to be patient, we find that His patience in us begins with prayer that springs forth from our drained, dispirited souls.

Surrendering Our Burdens to God in Prayer

"True faith is a coming to Jesus Christ to be saved and delivered from a sinful nature, as the Caananite woman came to him and would not be denied," observed William Law, eighteenth-century author of *A Serious Call to a Devout and Holy Life*. "It is a faith that in love and longing and hunger and thirst and full assurance will lay hold on Christ as its loving, certain and infallible Saviour."[2]

When mothering brings us to the end of ourselves, when we know beyond a shadow of a doubt that we cannot conjure up peace and patience independent from the Holy Spirit's gifting, when our hearts cry out for rest and strength in the midst of our daily lives as they are actually lived moment by moment, Jesus stands at the door and knocks. "Come unto Me," He says, as only our good Shepherd can—and prayer is where we meet Him.

Prayer is the vehicle we use to transport the loads that weigh heavily on our hearts, leaving them at the

If you are swept off your feet, it's time to get on your knees.
—FRED BECK

—— ❧ ——

The best prayers are often more groans than words.
—JOHN BUNYAN

—— ❧ ——

"I find it especially exasperating to parent older girls. I'd rather they stayed little!"
—SUSAN, AGE 38

—— ❧ ——

Every time you pray, if your prayer is sincere, there will be new feeling and new meaning in it which will give you fresh courage, and you will understand that prayer is education.
—FYODOR DOSTOYEVSKY

foot of the cross. In prayer, we turn to face God as we are, with longing, hunger, and thirst, asking to be filled again. Prayer is the entry point into the practice of patience, the means by which we surrender our burdens, accept our limitations, see the next step, and receive spiritual endurance to go on in God's strength rather than our own.

I realize this probably sounds familiar. More than likely, you have already spent uncounted hours praying on behalf of your family. Without prayer, you cannot picture what your life would be like, nor would you want to. You may be well acquainted with the Bible stories and Scripture verses regarding prayer, including these:

- "The eyes of the LORD are on the righteous and his ears are attentive to their cry. The righteous cry out, and the LORD hears them; he delivers them from all their troubles. The LORD is close to the brokenhearted and saves those who are crushed in spirit" (Ps. 34:15,17–18).

- "You are forgiving and good, O LORD, abounding in love to all who call to you. Hear my prayer, O LORD; listen to my cry for mercy. In the day of my trouble I will call to you, for you will answer me" (Ps. 86:5–7).

- "Pray all the time. Ask God for anything in line with the Holy Spirit's wishes. Plead with him, reminding him of your needs" (Eph. 6:18, TLB).

"Our first prayer needs simply to tell God, 'O God, help me to pray, because I cannot pray by myself,'" Dr. James Houston reminded us in his encouraging book *The Transforming Power of Prayer.* "Such a prayer helps us to recognize how prayer expresses our deepest need before the kingship of God."[3]

Prayer Works

Without a doubt, prayer is a mother's best haven. It is the safe place to which we retreat when we need to receive patience—*and* to ask for help, sustenance, and direction when our maternal influence appears to be ineffective. Incessantly interceding for our daughters in prayer is a uniquely Christian privilege, a responsibility that bears fruit in season, producing a timely harvest that also benefits future generations. "Aspire to God with short but frequent outpourings of the heart; admire His bounty; invoke His aid; cast yourself in spirit at the foot of the cross; adore His goodness; treat with Him of your salvation; give Him your whole soul a thousand times a day," Francis de Sales admonished.[4] This is an excellent summary of our much-needed maternal prayer plan, don't you think?

"I thought I knew how to pray, until my daughter reached adolescence and proved to me that there were vast regions of unexplored territory left to discover!" exclaimed my friend Cynthia. "I don't think I had ever prayed that much in my life. There were so many things I was anxious about, both real and imagined: school success, extracurricular activities, driving hazards, dating issues, disagreements about appropriate attire, the onset of PMS. . . . When hovering over Meg's shoulder was no longer possible, I realized how much I needed to depend on God to protect and guide my daughter. Through prayer, I find peace—and recover my sense of sanity in the process."

When we know that we have no real ability to control a particular problem or situation, prayer becomes our most important means of action. Here is a quick scriptural summary of why—and how—prayer works on our behalf in this regard:

When you get to your wit's end, you'll find God lives there.
—*ELIZABETH YATES*

— &⅘ —

Don't imagine that if you had a great deal of time you would spend more of it in prayer. Get rid of that idea! Again and again God gives more in a moment than in a long period of time, for his actions are not measured by time at all.
—*TERESA OF AVILA*

— &⅘ —

Prayer is the determination to be alone before God, with no gallery to play to and no distracting comparisons to make.
—*JAMES HOUSTON*

- *Prayer delivers protection from harm.* "Therefore let everyone who is godly pray to you while you may be found; surely when the mighty waters rise, they will not reach him" (Ps. 32:6).

- *Prayer lightens the load.* "To the LORD I cry aloud, and he answers me from his holy hill" (Ps. 3:4).

- *Prayer partners with thanksgiving.* "Be joyful always; pray continually; give thanks in all circumstances, for this is God's will for you in Christ Jesus" (1 Thess. 5:16–18).

- *Prayer brings wisdom.* "If any of you lacks wisdom, he should ask God, who gives generously to all without finding fault, and it will be given to him" (James 1:5).

- *Prayer promotes peace.* "Do not be anxious about anything, but in everything, by prayer and petition, with thanksgiving, present your requests to God. And the peace of God, which transcends all understanding, will guard your hearts and your minds in Christ Jesus" (Phil. 4:6–7).

- *Prayer puts our love for others into action.* "And this is my prayer: that your love may abound more and more in knowledge and depth of insight, so that you may be able to discern what is best and may be pure and blameless until the day of Christ, filled with the fruit of righteousness that comes through Jesus Christ—to the glory and praise of God" (Phil. 1:9–11).

- *Prayer defeats the opposition.* "Pray in the Spirit on all occasions with all kinds of prayers and requests. With this in mind, be alert and always keep on praying" (Eph. 6:18).

- *Prayer builds the spiritual strength of Christ's followers.* "We have not stopped praying for you and asking God to fill you with the knowledge of his will through all spiritual wisdom and understanding. And we pray this in order that you may live a life worthy of the Lord and may please him in every way: bearing fruit in every good work, growing in the knowledge of God, being strengthened with all power according to his glorious might so that you may have great endurance and patience, and joyfully giving thanks to the Father, who has qualified you to share in the inheritance of the saints in the kingdom of light" (Col. 1:9–12).

- *Prayer goes where we cannot go and does what we cannot do.* "We do not know what we ought to pray for, but the Spirit himself intercedes for us with groans that words cannot express. And he who searches our hearts knows the mind of the Spirit, because the Spirit intercedes for the saints in accordance with God's will" (Rom. 8:26–27).

- *Prayer recognizes who is in control.* "I call on you, O God, for you will answer me; give ear to me and hear my prayer" (Ps. 17:6).

"Prayer does not fit us for the greater works; prayer *is* the greater work," Oswald Chambers reminded us.[5] In practical terms, this means making prayer a top priority in our relationship with our daughters—as much a part of our responsibility to them as fixing their food, buying them clothing, getting good family medical care, providing sound discipline, and supervising their schooling.

When my daughters were young, I remember being especially exasperated by their ongoing sibling rivalry, which at times flared up in spite of every parenting skill and disciplinary measure I used to quench it. Nothing I did—and I did plenty—seemed

A vision without a task is a dream; a task without a vision is drudgery; a vision and a task is the hope of the world.
—ANONYMOUS

———— ✍ ————

Lord, make me an instrument of Your peace. Where there is hatred let me sow love; where there is injury, pardon; where there is doubt, faith; where there is despair, hope; where there is darkness, light; and where there is sadness, joy.

O divine Master, grant that I may not so much seek to be consoled as to console; to be understood as to understand; to be loved as to love. For it is in giving that we receive; it is in pardoning that we are pardoned; and it is in dying that we are reborn to eternal life.
—SAINT FRANCIS OF ASSISI

to make a difference for very long. Time and again, their colorfully clashing personalities and opposing temperaments sparked the latest Dispute of the Day, resulting in yet another round of hurt feelings on both sides. For years, I prayed that one day the girls would become good friends regardless of their surprisingly substantial differences. Though it appeared as if this were unlikely to happen, it finally did. Sometime during late adolescence, Joanna and Katherine declared a truce. The war was over. And though the peace is occasionally tested and may temporarily become a bit tenuous, I am happy to report that what once appeared to an anguished mother of preschoolers as only a desirable dream is now, years later, a much-prayed-for reality.

As we grow in the experience of mothering our daughters, we increasingly learn that prayer accomplishes the things we cannot carry out in ourselves—or in others. Through prayer, we find the strength to be quiet as we wait for the answers only God can give.

Putting It Into Practice

1. Write down your own definition of patience. Use several verses from the Bible as examples to back up your points, if you wish.

2. When your patience runs out, how do you think, act, and feel? Which well-known stress factors seem to make you more vulnerable to losing your patience with your family (fatigue, low blood sugar, lack of spousal support, PMS, overscheduling, etc.)? Do you see any patterns at work in your life that regularly set you and your daughter up for developing conflicts? What specific ways will you care for yourself as a way of preventing unnecessary "blowups" between the two of you?

3. Why is prayer "the entry point into the practice of patience"?

4. List five or more situations with your daughter that cause you to lose patience with her. Describe in detail what you would normally say and do in each circumstance. Are there any ideas you have in response to reading this chapter that you would like to use with your daughter the next time your patience starts to run out?

5. How has prayer helped you develop patience? Do you want to spend more time in prayer? In just a few sentences, tell the Lord what changes you would like to make in this vitally important area of your life; then ask Him to help you make this desire a reality.

6. What are some specific ways you can pray for your daughter? If you do not have a prayer journal, you may want to consider starting one as a way of prompting you to pray and for regularly recording your prayers (and the Lord's answers to them).

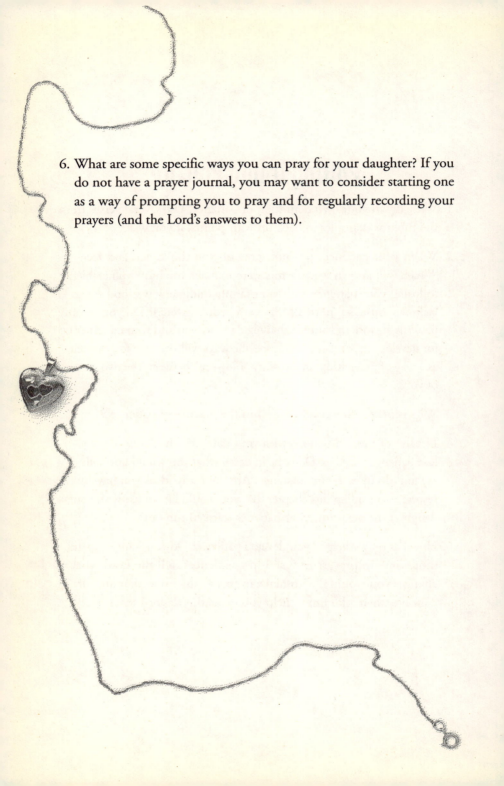

Who's in Control?

Let your understanding strengthen your patience. In serenity look forward to the joy that follows sadness.

—*Peter Damian*

Chapter Six

———— ❧ ————

When Jessica was born, Susan never imagined that she would find herself sitting in a hospital room with her daughter 16 years later, watching a nurse give Jessica an intravenous feeding for treating anorexia nervosa.

The condition, now life-threatening, first appeared in the guise of a simple weight-reduction diet. But after taking off the six pounds she had gained between Thanksgiving and New Year's, Jessie still hadn't felt thin enough. She liked the sense of control over her body that continuous dieting provided. The slender teen didn't mind eating next to nothing—in fact, she found she actually enjoyed it. It felt great to lose weight, and the thought of getting any larger was terrifying to her. Soon, nothing mattered more to her than staying thin.

Susan didn't grasp the extent of her daughter's physical and emotional crisis until she watched a made-for-television movie about adolescent eating disorders. That's when she realized that all the warning signs were there. Irritability. Lethargy. Brittle hair and bulky clothing. Excessive exercising. And unrelenting self-perfectionism. Susan phoned their family physician the following morning.

Both mother and daughter were shocked at the doctor's orders after hearing her diagnosis: immediate hospitalization that must continue until Jessica's condition was stabilized, followed by ongoing private counseling, family therapy, and peer group meetings. With Jessie's weight hovering well below 90 pounds, the cure wouldn't come overnight. Expert care and compassionate spiritual support were critically needed.

At the hospital, Susan prayed silently by Jessica's bedside: *Dear Father, revive Jessica's spirit as she begins the recovery process. Give her the grace to accept the doctor's treatment plan. Open her heart to Your loving will. In Jesus' name, bind every evil thing that has come against Jessie. I thank You for my daughter, Lord, and I release her into Your hands. Amen.*

As her feeling of helplessness slowly subsided, Susan looked into her daughter's eyes with renewed confidence and kept praying.

—— ✺ ——

Molly received the phone call about the accident shortly after 9:30 in the evening: Someone's pickup truck had slammed into the compact car her daughter Christina had been riding in with several friends from church.

"No one was killed," the police officer told her. "Your daughter's condition doesn't appear to be critical, but the extent of her injuries is still being determined. Is someone available to drive you to the emergency room right away?"

Memories, triggered by panic, flashed through Molly's mind: two-year-old Christina looking small and pale in the hospital bed after ear tube surgery; five-year-old Christina tumbling off the playground slide; 10-year-old Christina grimacing as Dr. Johnson sewed up a cut on her forehead caused by a wayward softball.

After calling her next-door neighbor for a ride, Molly sat down on the living room couch and asked God to touch her daughter, to guide the physician's hands, to guard Christina's life. Within a few minutes, an inexplicable peace covered her mind. Whatever the news turned out to be, Molly firmly believed Jesus was in control, and it was this knowledge that gave her the strength to stand and head toward the door when the doorbell rang.

— ❧ —

"Mom, I realize it's an awkward time for me to tell you this, but I thought you should know anyway. I'm breaking up with Eric because he pressured me into having sex with him and I feel really bad about it."

On the other end of the phone line, 600 miles away, tears filled Terry's eyes as she listened to her 19-year-old daughter, a college sophomore at a private Christian university.

"Are you still there, Mom?"

It wasn't a good time for the disclosure. Terry's husband, Pat, the senior pastor of a large Chicago congregation, was out of the country, leading a Christian outreach team on a nine-city, month-long tour of Russia and Eastern Europe. He wouldn't be home for 12 days. As usual, Terry's calendar had been packed: church committee meetings scattered throughout the month; exercise classes every other weekday; a Tuesday morning governor's prayer breakfast; Wednesday night Bible study; an unexpectedly long lunch with a prayer partner on Thursday; and today, Friday, a women's retreat Terry

God is like a mother who carries her child in her arms by the edge of a precipice. While she is seeking all the time to keep him from danger, he is doing his best to get into it.
—JOHN VIANNEY

— ❧ —

Praise be to God, who has not rejected my prayer or withheld his love from me!
—PSALM 66:20

— ❧ —

She flies by her own wings.
—LATIN PROVERB

— ❧ —

He has sent me . . . to bestow on them a crown of beauty instead of ashes, the oil of gladness instead of mourning, and a garment of praise instead of a spirit of despair.
—ISAIAH 61:1B,3

was to speak at in three hours. But was there *ever* a good time to receive this kind of heartbreaking news?

"Mom?"

Another second or two ticked by on the kitchen clock. Whatever Terry chose to say in the next few moments would be remembered for years to come, perhaps even for a lifetime.

Several phrases formed in Terry's mind, only to disappear. Finally, she prayed simply, *God, please give me the words. Thank You for Cara's openness. Help me to respond wisely.*

Recognizing Our Limits

These three vignettes represent one of the most difficult challenges we face as mothers: coping with the events and experiences we cannot control in our daughters' lives. When it comes to our children, we would do anything in our power to protect them from hurt and harm. But the number of life events and experiences that mothers may *influence* but cannot ultimately *control* concerning their children's lives is surprisingly substantial. On days when I am tempted to forget this, I sometimes reflect on this sizable list:

Events, Experiences, and Personal Traits I May Influence—
But Can't Control—in My Daughter's Life

• My pregnancy and the outcome of my daughter's birth

• Her personality and temperament

• Her aptitudes, skills, and abilities

• The rate of her physical, emotional, social, and spiritual development

• Her health and safety

• Her conversion to Christ

• Her level of academic achievement

- The use of her gifts and talents

- Her size and appearance

- Her abstinence from sex, drugs, and alcohol

- Her passions and preferences

- Her friends

- Her college and career choices

- Her financial and social status

- Her selection of a mate and the timing of her marriage

- Her childbearing and child-rearing choices

- Her state of happiness and emotional well-being

Though we may sometimes wish we could return to an earlier, simpler time when we could make things better with a single kiss, we can't. As our girls grow up, if our bond with them is to remain healthy, the maternal behaviors of the not-so-distant past must be replaced with new behaviors that recognize, support, and respect their developing individuality. We must shield our daughters from our anxieties and worries about them—and our frustration at being unable to manage their lives when things are not proceeding according to our plans. We cannot forever maintain the same level of influence over them that we enjoyed during the early stages of mothering. Understanding and accepting this truth should bring us to our knees and lead us to rely more deeply upon God's tender grace.

When a mother finally decides to give her daughter some advice, the mother usually learns plenty.

—EVAN ESAR

———— ✍ ————

Have no fear of sudden disaster or of the ruin that overtakes the wicked, for the LORD will be your confidence and will keep your foot from being snared.

—PROVERBS 3:25–26

———— ✍ ————

Let nothing disturb you. Let nothing terrify you. All things pass away. God is unchangeable. Patience gains everything. He who clings to God wants nothing. God alone is sufficient.

—TERESA OF JESUS

The Source of Our Strength

"My grace is sufficient for you, for my power is made perfect in weakness," declared the Lord to the apostle Paul (2 Cor. 12:9)—a lasting insight we are more likely to acquire during challenging life trials. When we are brought to the end of our ability to cope, we discover why surrendering and fighting back sometimes must take place simultaneously.

For me, this has happened over small, relatively unimportant things as well as in the midst of life-changing family upheavals. A toddler's bout with stomach flu at 4:00 in the morning or the missing blouse my teen borrowed without asking may provoke a sudden sense of helplessness or an immediate flash of anger—particularly on days when my energy is low, an important deadline is looming, and I find myself periodically bursting into tears for no reason.

I used to think that the Serenity Prayer sounded trite, until the day I paused long enough to consider the deep meaning in its simple message: "God, give us the grace to accept with serenity the things that cannot be changed, courage to change the things which should be changed, and the wisdom to distinguish the one from the other."[1]

The last part is where I tend to get stuck. I like to *make things better*. I prefer solving problems to letting problems get resolved, according to God's perfect timing, by the people who need to take responsibility for them. I do not like the squirmy discomfort I feel when I cannot fix circumstances to fit my expectations.

Needless to say, I require God's constant companionship and healing help if I am to live anywhere close to a state of serenity on a daily basis. In my ongoing efforts to understand, accept, and fulfill my heavenly Father's will, I sometimes feel overwhelmed by the scope and limitations of my vocation.

And yet, this is what has amazed me at critical turning points I've encountered while mothering my daughters: When I should have been the most afraid, God supplied vigorous courage. When I should have been completely confused, God provided holy wisdom. When I should have been totally exhausted, God sent life-giving strength.

This doesn't mean, of course, that I have never been afraid, confused, or exhausted. As a mother, I am well-acquainted with my manifold weaknesses. But I also have come to know the mysterious power that can arrive, without warning, at precisely the moment I least expect it—the wonder of being cared for by a compassionate Creator who keeps a special closeness with every mother in crisis. Like the women whose stories are told at the beginning of this chapter, I have been privileged to experience this most uncommon kind of comfort when I most needed it. Perhaps you have, too.

Giving Control to God

No matter how much we may wish we could gently guide the course of our daughters' lives to a guaranteed destination, we can't. That's God's job. And it's up to us to trust Him with it.

"I am constantly in need of God's strength and grace as I am learning to accept the decisions my daughter is making about her life," said my friend Barb. "It's a day-by-day experience, with some days going better than others. Reading the psalms has been particularly encouraging for me. Knowing I can be completely honest with God about the way I'm feeling enables me to trust Him more deeply—especially when Kristin closes herself off from me and spends time with friends I don't approve of."

"The number one help for me in resolving conflicts with my daughters is to take the issue to the Lord,"

"It grieves me when my daughters make poor choices for themselves against my advice or the teaching they have had."
—LINDA, AGE 38

While time lasts there will always be a future, and that future will hold both good and evil, since the world is made according to that mingled pattern.
—DOROTHY L. SAYERS

Humble yourselves, therefore, under God's mighty hand, that he may lift you up in due time. Cast all your anxiety on him because he cares for you.
—1 PETER 5:6–7

I avoid looking downward or backward, and try to keep looking upward.
—CHARLOTTE BRONTË

added Penny, the mother of two young women, ages 15 and 25. "He always directs me to just the right Scripture passage or leads me toward a creative idea to implement. He shows me where I am wrong or in error. When it's appropriate, I write letters to my daughters asking forgiveness or simply affirming my love and respect for them as God's children. I find that when *my* perspective is straight, I'm then able to listen with love as we discuss our current concerns."

Ann described several valuable insights gleaned from mothering her three adolescent daughters: "Talking, reviewing, and rewording are tools that my daughters and I have used to improve our communication skills. Mostly, though, we are committed to living in harmony and mutual support, so we keep working on areas of disagreement until we are united or, at least, accepting of one another's point of view. Sometimes it is helpful to leave a particularly painful subject alone for a while and let some inner healing take place before resuming work on the area of difficulty."

Knowing Our Limitations

The good news, of course, is that there are also many exciting and wonderful things that happen during our daughters' lifetimes. As their mothers, we become the thankful witnesses to a host of milestones, growth steps, celebrations, achievements, and significant turning points.

Wisdom leads us to understand that we cannot control these events either. Knowing our limitations means that we recognize God's handiwork in *every* moment, at each life stage, whether it is painful or pleasurable, happy or sad, easy or difficult, frustrating or satisfying. We realize that a person's life comprises a much larger, grander landscape than what is seen in the shifting patterns of day-to-day circumstances, current opinions, and sudden mood changes. Though we cannot view the entire picture yet, we can rest in the assurance that the Lord faithfully loves our daughters and is tenderly working for their good in even the tiniest details. The Painter is creating a priceless masterpiece. And we can trust Him to complete His job—perfectly.

But let's be honest: It is easier for most of us to believe that God is in control when things are going smoothly for our daughters. Certain kinds of conflicts and situations cause us to feel our maternal inadequacies as never before. At times, our direct intervention is needed, taking us into unexplored territory that no longer feels safe or comfortable for us. When Susan realized that her daughter, Jessica, had developed anorexia, additional support became vital. "Prayer helped me to face the necessity of treatment for Jessie, and prayer kept me going once the treatment began," Susan explained. "Beyond this, our doctor played a significant role in showing me what I could do to support my daughter's healing and recovery."

Knowing our limitations includes acknowledging the value of seeking professional and pastoral assistance when chronic eating disorders, a drug or alcohol habit, unplanned pregnancy, sexual abuse, depression, or any other serious concern becomes evident. Getting the help we need shows our daughters that we are not willing to tolerate harmful behaviors, that we cherish them enough to honestly face their pain, that we are not afraid to take responsibility for our part—and that we will leave with them their share of the responsibility for making necessary changes.

So, when the going gets rough, remember what these mothers—and many more—say helps them most:

- Read the psalms.

- Give your concerns to Jesus.

If you lose your heart about your work, remember that none of it is lost, that the good of every good deed remains and breeds and works on forever, and that all that fails and is lost is the outside shell of the thing.
—CHARLES KINGSLEY

———— ❧ ————

At each point of a child's growth, they leave us by degrees, and we must learn to give them again into God's hands.
—KAREN BURTON MAINS

———— ❧ ————

If a man is centered upon himself, the smallest risk is too great for him, because both success and failure can destroy him. If he is centered upon God, then no risk is too great, because success is already guaranteed—the successful union of Creator and creature, beside which everything else is meaningless.
—MORRIS L. WEST

- Do what you can.

- Consider what God's Word says.

- Get the support you need.

- Place your daughter in the Lord's hands.

- Keep praying.

We will find ourselves doing a significant amount of letting go over the long span of our daughters' lifetimes—accepting the things we cannot change, changing the things we can, and finding the wisdom we need, day by day, to know the difference. But we need not dread the transformation of our maternal influence with the onset of our daughters' emerging adolescence and adulthood. Nor should we fear the future.

As we acknowledge God's control over the course of our daughters' life choices, events, and experiences, we can open our hands and surrender the concerns and anxieties to which we cling. In exchange, we receive peace and the wisdom learned in letting go.

"When God began to make the world and put it in order and caused light to shine, it was a chaos, a state of utter confusion, without form, and void, and darkness was on the face thereof," wrote Jonathan Edwards in *Images or Shadows of Divine Things*. "So commonly things are in a state of great confusion before God works some great and glorious work in the church and in the world, or in some particular part of the church or world, and so oftentimes toward particular person."[2]

Isn't it comforting to remember that our heavenly Father has things under control even in the midst of chaos? That His compassionate design for our daughters' lives never wavers? That we can trust the Creator of the universe to accomplish what we cannot possibly do for our offspring?

We can count on this: God's love for our daughters exceeds our highest expectations, our fondest hopes, and our most fervent desires for their good—and no matter what today looks like, we can rest in knowing that His purposes for their lives cannot be thwarted.

Balancing Acts

1. On a sheet of paper, describe several turning points—for better or worse—in your relationship with your mother that took place during your teen years. Was your mother supportive, trustful, respectful, affirming? If so, how did she express these qualities? If not, what were the ways she showed her lack of support, trust, respect, or affirmation?

2. List the areas in your daughter's life that you would most like to control, if you could.

3. Look up several Bible passages that contain the admonitions "Do not fret," "Do not worry," and "Do not be anxious." Why are worry and anxiety destructive to our relationship with the Lord and our relationships with others?

4. When we give our fears to God, what does His Word promise He will give us in return?

5. As your daughter enters adolescence and adulthood—and increasingly distances herself from your influence—where will you obtain the prayer support and sound advice needed to help ease the transition?

Promoting Our Daughters' Sexual Well-Being

Truth, properly inculcated, can never be injurious. The only questions are, When and How?

—*Sylvester Graham*

Chapter Seven

———— ✿ ————

With three menstruating women in our family, life can get a little strange sometimes. I remember one month, not long ago, when my two daughters were both in bed—at the same time—with cramps. Both needed the heating pad, and it wasn't working. Both asked for medication to soothe their discomfort. Since Katy is allergic to aspirin, ibuprofen, and other anti-prostaglandins (today's best drug treatments for painful periods), she had to settle for a nonaspirin pain reliever. Unfortunately, this quickly proved ineffective, so I ran to the store to buy a hot water bottle and some red raspberry leaf tea—natural home remedies that had worked well for her in the past.

Why is it that, for years, I thought I was never going to stop having to buy disposable diapers and baby aspirin, only to discover a few years later that these "indispensable" items would soon be replaced by sanitary pads and medicine to relieve PMS?

To top it all off, upon further investigation I discovered that both girls weren't actually menstruating: one definitely was, the other definitely wasn't. (She was *ovulating*, which, she reminded me emphatically, causes her more discomfort than her periods do.) Lesson: "Cramps" is not simply a synonym for the kick-off phase of the menstrual cycle in our house; it can also be conveniently used to describe other momentous feminine occasions as well. At least I wasn't PMS-ing at the same time. Thankfully, that came later in the week.

These events—periods, ovulation, and PMS—have been recurring themes at our house for many years. Though you may find this surprising, the physiological rites of puberty, the "mystery language" of periods, and the fundamental realities of PMS have never been taboo topics around our kitchen table. Somehow my daughters and I have managed to talk about these topics—and many others related to the subject of human sexuality—while keeping our sense of humor and propriety intact. And we've learned a great deal from one another as a result.

In this chapter, you'll find a brief overview of information aimed at promoting your daughter's sexual well-being. The material on these pages is different from what you'll find in the other chapters. I've included it in *Kindred Hearts* because I feel strongly enough about this aspect of family life that I simply couldn't leave it out. What I offer here is not a detailed instruction manual, a complete course on abstinence education, or a guidebook on dating (all subjects worthy of their *own* books!)—it's a pep talk, plain and simple, based on my 20 years' experience teaching more than 7,000 students about women's sexuality through church groups, community college classes, expectant-parent instruction, university courses, and conference seminars. More important, the words I share here spring from my own experience of teaching my two daughters about human sexuality.

I realize that I can't tell you the when and how of sexuality education for your family any more than you can for mine. That is up to each mother to determine. So, take what you can use from this chapter and leave the rest. May the biological bond you share with your daughter bring you joy in the years ahead!

Thinking Back

PMS—treatable condition or disabling disease? *Menstruation*—monthly phenomenon or cyclical curse? *Sexual intercourse*—intimate marital encounter or dreaded duty? *Childbirth*—family event or fearsome feat? *Menopause*—life passage or incapacitating impairment? What's normal? What isn't? Who even wants to talk about these troublesome topics, anyway?

Think back for a moment on how you first learned about the varied facets of a woman's sexuality. Who told you? What did she say? How did you feel when you heard the news? Surprised? Shocked? Scared? Saddened? Or simply curious?

Some young women receive little maternal instruction, if any, about what may eventually take place within their bodies. When new milestones are reached, few feel fully prepared for them. Even fewer actually celebrate each occasion. Yet, for those of us looking back, the passages of womanhood—starting our periods, giving up our virginity, having a baby, becoming a mother—were all big events that heralded the appearance of a brand-new phase in our lives.

For those of us who were blessed to have capable mothers in this regard, we learned that a woman's sexuality is multidimensional and many hued—a

As the only girl, I was guarded with the vigor of a dragon-slaying St. George. Mother felt it was her duty to see that I came unscathed through the dating years. Whenever I walked up the block with a date, no matter what the hour, she would be at the window. I'd groan inwardly and wait for the familiar call "Is that you, Mary?" I'd want to reply, "No, it's Gunga Din." But her method was effective. No suitor ever got fresh, with that alert sentry standing 20 feet above his head.
—MARY HIGGINS CLARK

———— ✎ ————

Trust in the LORD with all your heart and lean not on your own understanding; in all your ways acknowledge him, and he will make your paths straight.
—PROVERBS 3:5–6

dramatic, often deeply satisfying voyage, replete with spectacular sunsets, colorful cloudbursts, swift-shifting undercurrents, and occasional stormy seas. We were taught, for example, that starting to menstruate is a momentous event, worth wondering about and waiting for.

When it happened, we had so many questions—and there was Mom to answer all of them, one by one. She helped us find the right pads or tampons to use, then calmly demonstrated how to use them. She talked openly about the importance of bathing daily and eating good food. She checked books out of the library and discussed them thoroughly. Above all, she avoided provoking feelings of shame or embarrassment about having periods, although we still found it strange at first. Blood on our underpants! What a shock! But Mom just smiled and made it all seem quite normal somehow.

Naturally, not all of us had mothers who were skilled at the fine art of mother-daughter communication. We might have been told about a woman's sexuality in crude or frightening terms—or not told about it at all. Starting our periods may have been a traumatic, rather than climactic, event. Monthly bleeding symbolized pain and/or punishment, and we usually hated it. Boys didn't have periods, so why did *we* have to? Eventually, we pushed aside our inner anguish in order to get on with our lives, all the while living in a body we had learned to dislike and distrust.

Most of us, however, find ourselves somewhere between these two extremes. Our moms were neither terribly helpful nor hurtful when it came to equipping us to live with our sexuality. For us, home learning about womanly biology happened haphazardly—a little here, a little there, and a lot of it a little too late. We grew up with mixed feelings about menstruation, cramps, sex, birth control, childbearing, menopause, and all the rest. On some days, everything seemed fine; on others, we wished we never had to bother with things like periods, PMS, and pregnancy.

With our own daughters, we have the perfect opportunity to improve our outlook. All it takes is a little memorization—and a lot of unlearning negative ways of looking at a positive thing: our bodies the way God created them.

Getting Started

Knowing the essential facts, instead of relying on hearsay, is a basic first step to becoming our daughters' primary sex educators. (The ability to smile when asked embarrassing questions about female sexuality is also tremendously beneficial.) We need to be on friendly terms with our own bodies before we can pass on healthy attitudes to our daughters. And having a healthy attitude requires that we achieve a balance: that we neither worship nor degrade our bodies; that we love them enough to care for, instead of abuse, them.

"One reason why Christian women have such a hard time accepting themselves, including their bodies, is because the idea still prevails that the spiritual and mental areas of our lives are somehow closer to God, more pleasing to him and more 'Christian' than the physical realm," explained family educator Ingrid Trobisch in *The Joy of Being a Woman.* "The more authentic our faith is, the more we are able to live at peace with our bodies. The more I succeed in accepting myself as a physical creature, the more I am able to live in harmony and peace with myself." [1]

Scripture tells us that our bodies are temples of God (1 Cor. 3:16), the place where the Holy Spirit resides (Rom. 8:11). We are entreated to employ our bodies thoughtfully and considerately for God's glory (Rom. 12:1). Living out these truths, and sharing

Our mothers are our most direct connection to our history and gender.
—HOPE EDELMAN

— ✍ —

Menstruation is the body's way of telling a girl that she is growing up . . . that she is not a child anymore . . . and that something very exciting is happening inside.
—JAMES DOBSON

— ✍ —

"I wish my mother had talked to me about sex and the emotions a teenager faces when she is in a boy-girl relationship."
—TANIA, AGE 30

— ✍ —

Life becomes much more difficult and complicated if we try to discover ourselves what is good and bad.
—WALTER TROBISCH

our insights with our daughters about how they apply to a woman's sexuality, is a tremendous responsibility.

We hear a lot these days about sex education in the public schools and why parents need to take a more active role in teaching their children about sexuality. Of particular concern are the high rates of premarital sex, teen pregnancy, abortion, and sexually transmitted diseases among adolescents.

As mothers, we are given the unparalleled opportunity to teach our daughters to honor and respect their feminine sexuality every day, from the moment they are born. I am absolutely convinced that one of the strongest threads God weaves into the mother-daughter bond is the biological identity we share—our ability to identify with each other's cycles of ovulation and menstruation, to understand the feminine side of conjugal sexuality, and to celebrate our mutual experiences related to maternity and motherhood.

This same-sex legacy that began with Eve has been passed down through the centuries to us. How will we live it out? Do we believe the Bible is correct in portraying women's wombs and breasts as blessings (Gen. 49:25), worthy of our honor and respect? If we do, we will not wait for society to warp this scriptural point of view—we will teach our daughters ourselves, from birth, that being created female in God's image is a *good* thing (Gen. 1:26–27,31).

Before getting started, commit your concerns and ideas to the Lord in prayer. Then pray again and again for your daughter's sexual well-being. Ask that she would be protected from evil and would make wise choices regarding her sexuality. Seek God's wisdom and the Holy Spirit's help as you share your knowledge about human sexuality. Become familiar with scriptures related to marriage, sexuality, procreation, and family life. By providing your daughter with sound reasons for valuing her sexuality—combined with prayer and reasonable boundaries—you will offer her excellent protection against harmful social influences and lifestyle behaviors.

Talking About Sexuality with Your Daughter

Learn the facts for yourself first. You don't need to be a doctor or have a Ph.D. in anatomy and physiology to understand how a woman's body works. A good medical dictionary will help you pronounce any unfamiliar words. Get comfortable with the terminology and understand the menstrual cycle first—the rest will come naturally.

Go slowly, one step at a time. As you prepare yourself to share information about sexuality with your daughter, remember it always makes good sense to follow a developmental teaching method. Provide factual information in terms your daughter can understand. Little girls should learn that they have a uterus, a vagina, and breasts, just as little boys are taught they have a penis. Practice saying the words aloud, if necessary, without blushing. At the right moment, during a bath, for instance, your daughter will begin naming her body parts. Such everyday situations present excellent—and appropriate—learning opportunities for both mom and daughter.

Answer questions as plainly and simply as possible, using words that make sense to your child. Each year brings new questions—and your child's increasing ability to understand the answers. Follow your daughter's natural learning progression. Long explanations about sexuality are unnecessary; they can actually raise more questions than existed previously.

Take each natural learning opportunity as it comes. Don't wait to present information about sexuality in

---

She speaks with wisdom, and faithful instruction is on her tongue.
—PROVERBS 31:26

— ❧ —

No one can better prepare a daughter for respecting and honoring her womanhood than her prepared mother can.

— ❧ —

Years to a mother bring distress
But do not make her love the less.
—WILLIAM WORDSWORTH

— ❧ —

The people who influence us most are not those who buttonhole us and talk to us, but those who live their lives like the stars in the heavens and the lilies of the field, perfectly simply and unaffectedly. Those are the lives that mould us.
—OSWALD CHAMBERS

the form of a major (and mutually embarrassing) "mother-daughter talk." Children learn best by example and real-life situations. Each day will present you with unique opportunities to teach your daughter about the wonder of the natural world, including the amazing design of her body.

For example, let's say your four-year-old daughter barges in on you while you're changing sanitary pads in the bathroom and says, "Mommy! What is that?" A simple, fact-based explanation such as the following is all you need to satisfy her curiosity and plant seeds of truth to cultivate over the next few years: "Amy, this is called a sanitary pad. Mommy uses these when she has her period. All girls have periods when they grow up. When you grow up, you'll have a period just like Mommy does."

Now, if Amy asks the next obvious question—"What is a period?"— then you may wish to say, "A period is something every woman's body does every month to get ready to have a baby."

See how easy it is? No need to get into all the rest of it yet—there will be time enough for discussing the various amazing details later.

Avoid ignoring your daughter's sexuality as if it were an unmentionable topic or a dirty thing—but don't go out of your way to emphasize it either. If one's sexuality is to be a natural part of life as God designed it to be, we need to find a balance. This happens quite easily if you let your daughter know she can ask you—her own mother—anything.

How will she learn that she can ask you anything? Treat her with respect and answer her questions without making her feel ashamed, foolish, silly, embarrassed, or stupid.

For instance, what if your 10-year-old daughter says, "Mom, if sex is so great, can I watch you and Dad do it sometime?" Although it might be tempting to show your shock, disgust, or embarrassment, always keep in mind that real-life situations bring the most teachable moments.

I don't know how you'd reply, but I know what *I* said, because one of my daughters asked this! Here was my reply: "Yes, honey, sexual intercourse is special. In fact, it's so special that Mom and Dad share it with one another but not with anyone else. That's because it's private: It belongs to just the two of us. I know you're really curious, but you're going to have to trust me on this one. When you grow up and get married, I know you'll want to be private with your husband, too."

My children know by experience that they can ask me anything and—this is especially important—that I am the only one who is smart (and kind) enough to answer all of their questions calmly—albeit sometimes with a little humor mixed in. I don't ever belittle them or tease them inappropriately when it comes to discussing human sexuality.

Use the show-and-tell method of health education. Never before have women had so many products and remedies to choose from! Use books, real feminine hygiene products and packet inserts, and simple, hand-drawn sketches to illustrate your points.

For example, make sure your daughter is well-prepared for her first period before the actual event takes place. Discuss and demonstrate the use of sanitary pads, pain relievers for cramps, daily bathing—even what to do with stained underwear or bedsheets. When your daughter starts her period, celebrate by baking her a cake, taking her out for ice cream, or buying her a pretty nightgown! It's a big occasion, worth remembering. Later, when reality sets in and topics such as PMS come up, you'll want your daughter to feel good about bringing her concerns to you.

Last, but not least, *include fertility appreciation along with education about menstruation.* By avoiding a

For Thou didst form my inward parts; Thou didst weave me in my mother's womb. I will give thanks to Thee, for I am fearfully and wonderfully made; wonderful are Thy works, and my soul knows it very well.
—PSALM 139:13–14, NASB

— ❧ —

"My mom made it clear from an early age that a woman's sexuality is God's creation, a gift to be cherished, honored, and enjoyed."
—PAMELA, AGE 24

— ❧ —

What do girls do who haven't any mothers to help them through their troubles?
—LOUISA MAY ALCOTT

— ❧ —

God commands you to pray, but he forbids you to worry.
—JOHN VIANNEY

single-focus approach to the menstrual cycle, you will give your daughter a valuable gift—one that our society cannot possibly give her: the gift of appreciating the life-giving nature of sexuality.

A woman's fertility is a gift that allows new life to enter creation through her body in a miraculous manner. Respect for human life also means proper respect for the human body, including respect for the gift of fertility through which our bodies are created. Rather than teaching our girls to fear menstruation, pregnancy, and childbirth, let's teach them to genuinely respect *life*—theirs, ours, and everyone else's.

Common Questions Girls Ask

Discovering the questions about human sexuality that girls and young women ask most often—in situations where they feel free to ask them—will help you get ready to answer your daughter's concerns. Thus, you will effectively demonstrate to your child that when it comes to talking about sex, parents really *do* know best.

Twenty-six-year-old Lisa's experience confirms this key reality:

> When my friends started talking about sex, I remember being really thankful that my mom had gone over the basics with me several years before. She used a picture book with drawings of a baby developing in the womb. I was so curious about what each organ was!
>
> Mom warmly presented the information in a very matter-of-fact, respectful way, without embarrassment. I think that, had she been reluctant to teach me about sexuality, I would have picked up on any uneasiness. As it was, it all seemed quite dignified yet *normal* to me—so much so that I didn't think about sexuality much afterward. At least, not until my fourth-grade friends brought it up. Hearing them use slang terms, squeal "Eeewww!" and pretend to throw up made me mad.
>
> "Why are you making such a big deal out of this?" I asked

them, adding, "My mom told me about sex a long time ago. It's the way God made us, and that's that." Then I stomped off.

When questions about sexuality surface, are you ready to respond wisely, as Lisa's mom did? As you read through the following list of today's most frequently asked questions, imagine your potential responses. Be prepared to revise these answers after further reading, study, and prayer. Also, keep these confidence-boosting guidelines in mind while planning possible replies:

- Think through your responses ahead of time.

- Stay calm when specific questions arise.

- Focus on an age-appropriate level of discussion.

- Convey respect for your daughter's thoughts and feelings.

- Center your teaching on God's design.

- Develop a dating plan.

Early Questions (Ages 2–6)

"What's this (specific organ or area)?"

"How do I know I'm a girl?"

"Why do you have breasts and I don't?"

"Why do you have hair down there?"

Laugh and grow strong.
—IGNATIUS OF LOYOLA

———— ❦ ————

One of the best reasons for parents to be the first to tell their children about sexual union in marriage is to prevent them from getting an initial impression that is distorted or destructive.
—STANTON L. AND
BRENNA B. JONES

———— ❦ ————

Because God is certainly not embarrassed that we are sexual creatures, neither should we be.
—MARY ANN MAYO

"Where do babies come from?"

"Does having a baby hurt?"

"Where does the baby's milk come from?"

"When will my breasts get bigger?"

"How did I get into (or out of) your tummy?"

"Are you glad I'm a girl?"

"Why do you wear makeup?"

"What does this (tampon, sanitary pad, condom) do?"

"What's a belly button for?"

"Why did God make me a girl?"

"Why do you hug and kiss Daddy and me but not other people?"

Questions Older Girls May Ask (Ages 7–12)

"What does 'having sex' mean?"

"Why do people get married?"

"Did you and Dad have sexual intercourse in order to have me?"

"How does a baby stay alive before it's born?"

"What is an abortion? Is it wrong to have one?"

"How will I know when my period starts?"

"What does the word _____ (slang or obscene term) mean?"

"What happens during menstruation? Are periods painful?"

"Why are some children adopted and others aren't? Am I adopted?"

"Is it wrong to hold hands with a boy?"

"What is a virgin? Why is virginity important?"

"Can babies really grow in test tubes? How?"

"How do mothers' breasts make milk? Does breast milk taste different from cows' milk?"

"Do boys have periods? Why do girls have periods and boys don't?"

"Why are my friend's breasts getting bigger and mine aren't?"

Questions Teens May Ask (Ages 13–17)

"Can anyone get AIDS? How would I know if I had it?"

"What is a condom for?"

"Why do men look at *Playboy* magazine? Is it wrong? What is pornography?"

"What is a homosexual? What is a lesbian?"

"How old do I need to be before I can start dating?"

Questions. Your child's face turned up expectantly. The answer you give or don't give will color that child's thinking for the rest of his or her life. You have the possibility of laying foundations now for an entire lifetime.
—SUSAN SCHAEFFER
MACAULAY

— ✎ —

Watch your step. Stick to the path and be safe. Don't sidetrack; pull back your foot from danger.
—PROVERBS 4:26–27,
TLB

— ✎ —

Good habits are not made on birthdays, nor Christian character at the new year. The workshop of character is everyday life. The uneventful and commonplace hour is where the battle is lost or won.
—MALTBIE D.
BABCOCK

"What is a cesarean section?"

"Why shouldn't a couple live together before marriage?"

"Does it hurt to have sex?"

"What is the Pill, and what does it do?"

"Is masturbation a sin?"

"What is rape? Is a date rape a *real* rape?"

"Why do some people believe it's wrong to practice birth control?"

"Did you and Dad have sex before you were married?"

"What is an orgasm?"

"If my boyfriend wants to kiss me, what should I do?"

"What is a wet dream? Do girls have wet dreams?"

"What is incest?"

"Is it wrong to kiss your boyfriend? How far is too far?"

Immunizing our daughters against damaging worldviews by teaching them *our* views and values starts early and continues until adulthood—part of a lifelong conversation on how we live with our bodies as redeemed women in a fallen world. By instilling truth into their young minds and setting sound boundaries for their extracurricular activities, we lovingly inoculate our children against devastating social diseases, bolster their spiritual defenses, and promote their sexual health. *We are the best people for this task. No one can better prepare a daughter for respecting and honoring her womanhood than her prepared mother can.*

Breaking the Silence of Sexual Abuse

In recent decades, there has been a virtual explosion of information regarding childhood sexual abuse. Some specialists cite the statistic that one in every four girls will be sexually abused before she turns 18 years old; other experts claim the rates are significantly higher.[2] Though it's natural to want to tune out the disturbing reports we hear, we cannot deny that sexual abuse exists throughout the country and that it affects thousands of girls every year.

Generally, most sexual abuse starts when girls are between six and nine years of age, a time when many girls are easily convinced to stay silent about what's happening. Because most sexual abuse takes place inside a child's home or extended family, alert mothers can act as the first line of defense against harm. We do this by:

- Teaching our daughters the difference between good and bad touches.

- Understanding the signs of sexual abuse and assault.

- Immediately removing our daughters from situations in which sexual topics, gestures, jokes, references, and comments are creating an unhealthy or uncomfortable atmosphere.

- Responding quickly and lovingly in the unfortunate circumstance that abuse has already taken place.

Baby boomers who experimented with drugs and sex often have difficulty asking their own children to abstain. What can a parent do? Be honest about what you did wrong, teach abstinence, and let your children know you want to spare them the pain.
—BRENDA HUNTER

———— ❧ ————

"I haven't talked to my mom about sex since the little book she read to me in the second grade—and I'm married. I wish she could have been more open about what sex was all about, not to mention all the 'in-betweens.' I ended up falling into things rather than having an actual knowledge of 'if you do this, he'll want to do this.'"
—SARAH, AGE 26

Defining Sexual Abuse

In his book *The Wounded Heart*, Dr. Dan Allender defined sexual abuse as "any contact or interaction (visual, verbal, or psychological) between a child/adolescent and an adult when the child/adolescent is being used for the sexual stimulation of the perpetrator or any other person."[3] According to Dr. Allender, there are two levels of childhood sexual abuse. The first level, *sexual contact,* involves any type of intentional touch that physically or emotionally brings about sexual desire in the victim and/or the abuser. Abusive physical touch ranges from least severe (sexual kissing, fondling a fully clothed body) to most severe (forced or nonforced sexual intercourse, oral or anal sex). Whenever abuse involves sexual touch, at any level, far-reaching physical, emotional, and spiritual aftereffects occur.

The second level of sexual abuse defined by Dr. Allender is *sexual interactions.* Abusive sexual interactions between adults and children (or between older and younger children) are much more subtle than sexual abuse that involves illicit physical contact. This type of sexual abuse often takes place independently of sexual contact and, as a result, is less easily recognized. Repeated use of sexual language, exposure to pornographic magazines or videos, inappropriate attention directed toward a child's developing body, sexual comments, intrusive interest in a child's entry into puberty, and the intentional display of an adult's nude or partially dressed body are all examples of inappropriate sexual interactions.

"The fact that sexual abuse can be subtle ought not to cloud our perspective that it is equally abusive and damaging," Dr. Allender emphasized.[4] As mothers, let's not discount our intuitive sense that "something isn't right," even though a specific situation may involve a trusted friend or family member. If we hear or see an unacceptable visual, verbal, or psychological sexual interaction start to happen, it is essential that we remove our daughters from the scene without hesitation—or apology.

Recognizing the Symptoms

Since we cannot count on our daughters to recognize or report inappropriate or abusive behaviors they might encounter, it is up to us to become familiar with the emotional signs and physical symptoms associated with sexual abuse, including these:

- Unusual knowledge of sexual terms and facts

- Fear of being alone with previously trusted persons

- Abrupt change in personality

- Running away from home for no apparent reason

- Regular nightmares about a specific person

- Explicit sex play with other children

- Fear of being alone in the bathroom, basement, or some other secluded site (common sexual abuse locations)

- Excessive masturbation or other form of sexual self-stimulation

- Noticeable change in appetite or sleeping habits

- Seductive behavior and/or apparel

- Wearing too much clothing to bed or on warm days

- Social withdrawal, moodiness, or an inordinate amount of crying

- Fear of being alone with men or boys

Do not be wise in your own eyes; fear the LORD and shun evil. This will bring health to your body and nourishment to your bones.
—PROVERBS 3:7–8

— ✍ —

Sexually abusive words produce the same damage as sexually abusive contact. Yet the potential for minimization or feeling weird for being damaged makes the potential for change even more difficult for those more subtly abused than for those more severely abused.
—DAN B. ALLENDER

— ✍ —

To escape the distress caused by regret for the past or fear about the future, this is the rule to follow: leave the past to the infinite mercy of God, the future to his good providence; give the present wholly to his love by being faithful to his grace.
—JEAN-PIERRE DE CAUSSADE

- Sudden extreme shyness associated with bathing and/or dressing

- "Acting out": aggressive or violent behavior; sexualized behavior

- Return to infantile behaviors (thumb-sucking, clinging, bed-wetting, separation anxiety, etc.)

- Appearance of gifts or money not accounted for by birthdays or holidays

- Development of chronic physical ailments, such as headaches, pelvic pain, or digestive problems

- Sexually transmitted disease

- Unexplained or repeated bladder infections

- Pregnancy

- Genital/anal pain or itching

- Vaginal discharge, bleeding, or offensive odor

- Trouble with walking or sitting

- Stained, bloody, or damaged underwear, clothing, or linens [5]

Some victims of sexual abuse show many—or none—of the obvious signs of trauma. Because most of the signs are also associated with other causes, the bulk of this list is not an absolute confirmation of sexual abuse. For this reason, it is especially important that you seek additional help in diagnosing symptoms you feel uneasy about.

What You Can Do

Any sign of emotional upset or physical trauma in your daughter should be taken seriously. If you think there is a chance that a problem exists, there are several things you can do:

1. *Believe your daughter and convey this belief to her.* This is very important. Children seldom lie about sexual abuse.

2. *Talk to your daughter in private.* Ask her to tell you what happened in her own words. Listen carefully, and don't press for details, especially if she is upset. You only need to get a general picture of what took place. And—this is very important—don't attempt to confront the abuser in the child's presence.

3. *Remain calm.* Your child's response may depend on how you handle the situation. If you stay calm and confident, you will reassure your daughter that what happened wasn't her fault and that she can trust you.

4. *Tell your daughter that she did the right thing by telling you about what happened.* Say that you're sorry she was hurt, that you know she is scared, and that you will protect her from further abuse. Girls are often coerced into promising not to tell about sexual contact or interaction, and she may feel guilty for breaking her promise to the abuser. She may also feel worried about, or be afraid of, getting the abuser into trouble. You may want to say that abusing children is a sickness and that the person will need help to get better. Though it is natural for you to want the person punished, your daughter may be deeply upset by hearing such talk. It is enough for her to know that the abuser did something wrong and will not be permitted to do it again.

All of us know someone who has suffered from sexual wounding. If we are not that someone, then it may be our daughter, son, neighbor, or the young wife from the Monday morning Bible study.
—*ALFRED ELLS*

—— ❧ ——

We are well aware of the pervasiveness of evil. We are not so foolish as to imagine that society will ever become perfect before Christ comes and establishes the fullness of his rule. . . . Nevertheless, we also believe in the power of God—in the power of God's gospel to change individuals and in the power of God's people (working like salt and light) to change society.
—*JOHN STOTT*

—— ❧ ——

Too much and too little education hinder the mind.
—*BLAISE PASCAL*

5. *Report the abuse.* State laws require caregiving adults to report suspected child abuse to law enforcement personnel or social service/protective service workers. Such reports may be made anonymously. If you suspect that penetration has occurred, seek medical attention right away and confidentially report your concerns to your daughter's physician.

6. *Call for help.* Contact a Christ-centered agency that has expertise in the field of sexual abuse. Since you probably haven't been trained to deal with this situation, the wisest thing you can do is to get in touch with professionals who can provide you and your daughter with compassionate, caring help. If you live in an isolated area, call Focus on the Family at 1-800-A-FAMILY for a phone referral to a qualified pastor or counselor in your area.

7. *Take whatever steps are necessary to protect your child from additional abuse.* For the time being, it is important to create a safe environment while you and your daughter begin the healing process. If the abuser lives in your home, see that *he* leaves—not your daughter. Or you may want to move out with your daughter. Separation from the abuser does not preclude the hope of family reconciliation. Though this may be possible at some point in the future, your immediate concern is for your daughter's protection and well-being.

It is our responsibility to teach our daughters about sexual abuse prevention and, in the heartbreaking event that intervention becomes necessary, to act as their loving advocates and protectors. Our daughters are depending on our sensitive support and prayerful supervision.

In Conclusion

In this chapter, I have suggested a number of ideas you can use as you introduce your daughter to God's amazing design for her life and cooperate with her Creator in guarding her from harm. But it's only a start.

I encourage you to stay available as a resource for your daughter for many years to come. As mothers, we are uniquely equipped to promote our daughters' sexual well-being on a lifelong basis—not just with anatomical facts and persuasive statistics, but with the changeless truth of Scripture to inspire and support their life choices.

As authors Stanton and Brenna Jones explained in their thought-provoking book *How and When to Tell Your Kids About Sex*: "Education about sexuality goes beyond providing information that is accurate and timely. We must also shape the values and attitudes of our kids, shape their worldview, practice what we preach (modeling), provide our children with the emotional strength they will need to make godly decisions, and instill in them the skills to implement the good decisions they make." They added, "Most importantly, their behavior will spring from their hearts, which will be informed by their personal relationship and devotion to God." [6]

The character building that begins when our daughters are still in their cradles continues through their formative years and beyond as we recognize everyday opportunities for shaping their characters and teaching them about the Bible's precepts for marriage and family life. With God's help and our instruction, our daughters will learn memorable lessons about God's good purposes for them: "'For I know the plans I have for you,' declares the LORD, 'plans to prosper you and not to harm you, plans to give you hope and a future. Then you will call upon me and come and pray to me, and I will listen to

There is so much to teach, and the time goes by so fast.
—ERMA BOMBECK

What is nobler than to rule minds or mould the character of the young? I consider that he who knows how to form the youthful mind is truly greater than all painters, sculptors, and all other of that sort.
—JOHN CHRYSOSTOM

You have made us for yourself, and our heart is restless till it rests in you. Who will grant me to rest content in you? To whom shall I turn for the gift of coming into my heart so that I may forget all the wrong I have done, and embrace you alone, my only good?
—SAINT AUGUSTINE

you. You will seek me and find me when you seek me with all your heart'" (Jer. 29:11–13).

By emphasizing that we passionately care about our daughters' characters, that we are sincerely concerned about the impact of their decisions on their lives, and that we are unafraid to intervene in order to protect them from harm when necessary, we provide vivid glimpses of God's unchanging love for them in *all* circumstances.

Practice Run

1. Write a brief description about the ways you learned about the "facts of life." Include your age, where you were, who told you, what the "message" about sexuality was (the values, information, and attitudes shared), and how you reacted. Reflect on the impact these revelations had upon your thinking about the many dimensions of a woman's sexuality: menstruation, PMS, ovulation, lovemaking, pregnancy, childbirth, breast-feeding, and menopause. Were your experiences positive or negative? Would you have preferred to receive your education at a different time or from someone else? If not then, when—and from whom?

2. As you grew older, what sources supplemented your learning about your body? Which were the most helpful? Were there any that were harmful? Looking back, is there anything you would change or do differently regarding your sexuality education?

3. Condense the ideas in this chapter that you plan to use in teaching your daughter about her sexuality. Are there any questions or topics you might find difficult to discuss? Which ones? How will you prepare yourself to fulfill your responsibility as your daughter's primary sexuality educator in these areas? Summarize your plan on a separate sheet of paper, using the following list as a guide:

   - My daughter's education about marriage and human sexuality will begin/began at the age of: _____.
   - I plan to teach her about the following topics according to the ages listed below:

Infancy to three years old:

Four to six years old:

Seven to nine years old:

10 to 12 years old:

13 to 15 years old:

16 to 18 years old:

4. As you read through the section in this chapter on childhood sexual abuse, did any specific scenes or situations from your life come to mind? If you know, or suspect, that sexual abuse occurred at some point in your past, what will you do (or have you done) to promote healing?

5. List several practical ways you will protect and promote your daughter's sexual innocence.

6. When your daughter asks you for guidelines about dating, at what ages will you start allowing her to participate in these activities?

Boy/girl church youth group: _____ *(age)*

Boy/girl parties (attend with friends): _____ *(age)*

School dances (attend with friends): _____ *(age)*

School sporting events (attend as a couple): _____ *(age)*

School dances (attend as a couple): _____*(age)*

*Going out with mixed-sex group on date
 (chaperoned)* _____*(age)*

*Going out with mixed-sex group on date
 (unchaperoned):* _____*(age)*

Going on double dates (chaperoned): _____*(age)*

Going on double dates (unchaperoned): _____*(age)*

Going on dates as couple (chaperoned) _____*(age)*

Going on dates as couple (unchaperoned) _____*(age)*

The Greatest Is Love

In a word, there are three things that last forever: faith, hope, and love; but the greatest of them all is love.

—1 Corinthians 13:13, NEB

Chapter Eight

———— ❧ ————

"*D*ebra? . . . Debra, is that you?"

The woman's voice on the other end of the line sounded familiar—and frantic.

"Yes, it's me," I answered, still wondering who was calling.

"It's Mrs. Swanson. How have you been?"

"I've been very well, thanks," I replied cordially.

My former Girl Scout leader's distinctive southern drawl, modified by years of midwestern living, immediately brought to mind a clear picture of her amiable face. Though it had been at least three years since I had seen her, I didn't have any trouble remembering Dolores Swanson.

"Have you heard from Sandra?" Mrs. Swanson asked.

Because her daughter and I had talked recently, I suspected that I knew the reason for the early morning phone call.

"As a matter of fact, I heard from Sandy just a few weeks ago. Is anything wrong?"

"Well, her father and I are concerned. She may have told you about the strict religious group she has joined. They call themselves God's Children," Mrs. Swanson explained, her voice trembling. "Sandra says she can't have any more contact with us. Apparently, members of the group have been given precise orders to cut off all communication with their families. They also told her to give all of her possessions and cash to them."

Mrs. Swanson paused, then said, "Mr. Swanson and I are deeply troubled by this situation. It seems that the only way we can help Sandra is to persuade her to leave the group, but we have no idea where she is right now. Can you help us?"

I understood why Mrs. Swanson was worried about her daughter. I was worried, too. Sandy and I had both become active Christians after graduating from high school the previous year. Now Sandy was heading in a different direction: After hearing about God's Children, she had moved into their living quarters in downtown Detroit, believing that the group would enable her to serve Christ on a full-time basis as she ministered to others through prayer, evangelistic street outreach, and sharing household tasks.

From what little I knew about God's Children, I felt uneasy about my friend's entry into a possibly dangerous cult. It also seemed bizarre that the group's local leaders were telling members not to have any family contact when everything I knew about the Bible promoted family reconciliation. I knew Sandy well enough to know she would not agree with this idea if she were thinking clearly.

I told Mrs. Swanson that I was willing to help in whatever way I could. As we discussed setting up a "rescue"—a surprise meeting in which Sandy's parents would pick up their daughter under false pretenses from the cult's headquarters and take her home—I asked God to give me wisdom. At 18 years of age, I was not accustomed to revealing my friends' secrets to their parents, and I did not feel entirely comfortable with telling Sandy's whereabouts to her mom. But I trusted Mrs. Swanson, and I knew she and her husband were acting in their daughter's best interests. So I provided the information that would help them bring Sandy home.

Though I am uncertain how much Mrs. Swanson eventually disclosed to her daughter about my participation in the rescue, Sandy and I remained friends. Within days of her tumultuous departure from the group, we were sitting on the floor in her bedroom, talking about her parents' bold intervention strategy and praying together about our future in the Lord.

What I did not know then—what none of us knew—was that Mrs. Swanson would joyously discover a personal relationship with Christ during this family crisis. Nor did we know that she would die suddenly as the result of a tragic car accident only a few months later.

More than 26 years have gone by since Mrs. Swanson called me and straightforwardly shared her concerns about Sandy. I will never forget her tenacious determination to protect her daughter from spiritual harm; nor have I ceased to marvel at the unique expression of God's providence that forever bonded this exceptional mother and her daughter together in Christ.

But what if Sandy had not cooperated with her mother's timely intervention in her life? What if she had refused to go home and stayed with the cult instead? What if she had decided not to speak to her parents after the rescue took place? What if my friend had chosen to hate or reject her mom?

I can still feel my mother's arms around me, holding me, as she stood out on the porch and we watched a storm come rolling across the lake, waves swelling, thunder crashing, lightning slicing the sky, and my mother telling me how beautiful it was. I found out later she was scared to death, but she taught me not to be afraid; I was safe in those arms.

—BETTY FORD

—— ✑ ——

Thou art my shield and hiding-place; I hope for the fulfillment of thy word.
—PSALM 119:114, NEB

—— ✑ ——

There is no room for fear in love; perfect love banishes fear.
—1 JOHN 4:18, NEB

—— ✑ ——

Love is more than a characteristic of God; it is His character.
—ANONYMOUS

I feel certain that Mrs. Swanson carefully weighed these risks, and many others, before confronting her daughter with her concerns. Her final course of action, however, was not ultimately affected by what others might do, say, or think. Dolly Swanson knew—and loved—her daughter better than anyone else. And that love, combined with God's gentle guidance and protective power, proved irresistible to Sandy at precisely the moment she most needed it.

Fearless Love

Loving our daughters with the Lord's love means loving them fearlessly, as Dolly Swanson did Sandy. To do this, Mrs. Swanson discovered, a mother must first face, and then surrender, her own fears to God.

Sharing our faith with our daughters acknowledges that we are willing to go the distance with them, no matter where it takes us. Following this path requires some degree of personal sacrifice. But it does not require constant worry, martyrlike thinking, or overcontrol. And, thankfully, the journey was not designed to be taken alone: Staying close to Jesus every step of the way ensures that we remain on the right road.

As Mother Teresa wisely said, "We all long for heaven where God is, but we have it in our power to be in heaven with Him right now—to be happy with Him at this very moment. But being happy with Him now means: loving as He loves, helping as He helps, giving as He gives, serving as He serves, rescuing as He rescues, being with Him for all the twenty-four hours, touching Him in His distressing disguise."[1] Her tender picture of discipleship also fittingly applies to loving, helping, giving to, serving, rescuing, being with, and touching our daughters. The key to this process, it seems to me, is *staying close to the Lord:* drawing upon His strength, trusting His Word, praying in His name, going where He leads, being living examples of His love—according to how and when He directs us to act.

In the early years of our children's lives, we share our love for Jesus through Bible instruction, home teaching, church attendance, caring for the sick, talking about God, saying prayers together, giving to the poor, and other important ways. We become accustomed to being their leaders, to looking back at our girls, fully expecting to find them following close behind. Then, one day, we discover that they are no longer there: They have matured enough to want to learn from a teacher of their own choosing, to form their own set of ideas and opinions, to believe what they decide they want to believe instead of unquestioningly accepting our beliefs as their own.

Discipling a daughter throughout her adolescence and into adulthood requires considerable prayer, perceptiveness, and patience. This is not necessarily an easy task, especially if she dons the "distressing disguise" of pop culture, or is engaged to marry an agnostic man, or starts smoking trendy cigars, or joins a weird religious sect.

"You can do nothing with children unless you win their confidence and love by bringing them into touch with oneself, by breaking through all the hindrances that keep them at a distance," asserted John Bosco, a nineteenth-century Christian known for his international youth ministry. "We must accommodate ourselves to their tastes, we must make ourselves like them."[2]

To bring them into touch with ourselves and break through all the hindrances that keep them at a distance, must we really accommodate ourselves to their tastes and make ourselves like them? Yes—in the sense that we are to understand our daughters, compassionately caring for and about them. This sounds remarkably similar

The greatest happiness of life is the conviction that we are loved—loved for ourselves, or rather, loved in spite of ourselves.
—VICTOR HUGO

———— ✍ ————

What is Christian perfection? Loving God with all our heart, mind, soul and strength.
—JOHN WESLEY

———— ✍ ————

"It wasn't until I became the mother of a teenage daughter that I gained an appreciation of why Mom and I disagreed so much during my adolescent years."
—DIANE, AGE 46

———— ✍ ————

Have Thine own way, Lord, have Thine own way. Thou art the Potter, I am the clay; mould me and make me after Thy will, while I am waiting, yielded and still.
—ADELAIDE T. POLLARD

to the strategy Jesus used when the Pharisees accused Him of befriending the wrong people. He knew that giving consideration to others and being close to them did not confer automatic approval of their likes and dislikes. Nor did it mean He imitated or accepted their behavior.

When we try to apply this same principle to our daughters, however, it does not always work. More often than not, we are apt to find it more than a little unsettling to have them question our beliefs, ideals, values, and notions of propriety. We may find ourselves, quite naturally, wanting our daughters to continue following our example—to believe the way we believe—even though we realize this is a totally unrealistic, and even unhealthy, expectation for our maturing children. As a result, opportunities for loving our daughters can be lost.

Keeping our perspective helps. Knowing that God isn't finished with our daughters, or with us, is a powerful reminder of the daily growth that is constantly taking place.

"The lump of clay, from the moment it comes under the transforming hand of the potter is, during each day and hour of the process, just what the potter wants it to be at that hour or on that day, and therefore pleases him; but it is very far from being matured into the vessel he intends in the future to make it," Hannah Whitall Smith explained in her classic book, *The Christian's Secret of a Happy Life.* "The little babe may be all that a babe could be, or ought to be, and may therefore perfectly please its mother; and yet it is very far from being what the mother would wish it to be when the years of maturity shall come."[3]

We tend to expect a great deal from our still-growing daughters. We want them to be God-pleasing, faith-filled, prayer-oriented, Word-wise, self-controlled, smart, responsible, respectful, healthy, happy, generous, well-groomed, kind, capable, and content with what they have. But God isn't finished with them yet. The Potter's work is far from completion. Are we daily trusting Him with our daughters' design? Do we believe that He is bringing them ever closer to being conformed to the image of His beloved Son?

We can live in hopeful expectation of our daughters' future glory knowing this: God will not abandon the work of His hands that He began at their conception. "The one who calls you is faithful and he will do it" (1 Thess. 5:24).

So, when we find ourselves getting tired and frustrated, we can recall what daughters say they need most from their mothers during their spiritual shaping process: They need us to rediscover our joy and delight in them, to see them as they will one day be. They need us to set and keep healthy boundaries with them. They need our friendship, caring, and compassion. They need our tenderness. They need our love.

A Loving Witness

It is easy to talk about loving our daughters. But learning how to love them in the way the Bible teaches is only possible when we set aside our self-centeredness, become quiet, and listen to the Lord.

When I need God's help in loving someone, I turn to 1 Corinthians 13 and read the oft-quoted passage beginning with the words "Love is . . ." Concen-trating on each part, I ask the Lord to help me love according to what the Bible says about love in this familiar paragraph, thinking about what it means in practical terms to charitably serve the person I am finding it difficult to love. Though I've committed the passage to memory, I always look at the words, mulling them over in my mind.

Using the New English Bible translation, I consider each phrase separately:

Joy is prayer—joy is strength—joy is love—joy is a net of love by which you can catch souls. She gives most who gives with joy.
—MOTHER TERESA

———— ✍ ————

I am thy servant; give me insight to understand thy instruction.
—PSALM 119:125, NEB

———— ✍ ————

When Mother taught us the Lord's Prayer, she put her heart into it. You tried to say it as she did, and you had to put a little of your own heart into it. I believe that Mother, realizing that she was left alone to raise three girls, knew that she had to have a support beyond herself.
—MARIAN ANDERSON

———— ✍ ————

Let love and faithfulness never leave you; bind them around your neck, write them on the tablet of your heart.
—PROVERBS 3:3

Love is patient;
  love is kind and envies no one.
Love is never boastful, nor conceited, nor rude;
  never selfish, not quick to take offense.
Love keeps no score of wrongs;
  does not gloat over other men's sins,
  but delights in the truth.
There is nothing that love cannot face;
  there is no limit to its faith, its hope, and its endurance.
Love will never come to an end. (1 Cor. 13:4–8)

I may read the passage three, six, even 10 times. Usually, a couple of problem areas leap out, as if highlighted in bold—the specific qualities of love about which the Lord is prompting me to more deeply depend upon Him. In confessing my sins and my shortcomings to God, I get at least a glimpse of why love has been lacking in the relationship. Then, with a better understanding of how God's strength and my weakness are a fitting combination, I ask the Lord to love the person through me. I learn something every time I do this. And I find that I need to do it often.

Loving with Christ's love—solid, strong, and steadfastly courageous—produces growth not only in our daughters but in us. As we sit in silence with God, openly admitting where we have failed or fallen short, we receive His forgiveness. Realizing that we cannot create for ourselves, or for our daughters, the kind of caring only Jesus can offer, we wait upon the outpouring of our Lord's love, believing His promise that our empty cups will be filled.

How many times per day (or week or month or year) we need to do this will depend on the emotional, spiritual, physical, and relational challenges we are facing. This requires conscious effort on our parts, a deliberate setting aside of time, thought, and energy separate from everything else on our full agendas. But, according to the Bible, "love is the greatest of them all," and if we believe it, we will make loving God, our families, and one another the top priority in our lives.

When it comes to sharing Christ with our daughters, sharing His love is the best witness to the reality of His redemption that we have to offer.

Creation seems to be delegation through and through. He will do nothing of Himself which can be done by creatures. I suppose that is because He is a giver.
—C. S. LEWIS

———— 🙰 ————

We don't come out of the womb devaluing love.
—JOHN TOWNSEND

Love Lessons

1. Think back to when you were growing up and what you were taught about God. Was the Bible discussed and talked about openly within your family? How were you introduced to Christ? What did your parents believe about Jesus? Did prayer play a visible role in your household? Was going to church something you enjoyed, dreaded, or endured?

2. On a separate sheet of paper, make a list of the spiritual truths, principles, values, and doctrines your mother taught you by her words and example. Which of these teachings have had the greatest impact on your life? Circle the beliefs your mother held that you still consider to be true and continue to live by; cross out any you have revised or rejected since becoming an adult.

3. Describe your most memorable moment spent with your mom in Christ's presence.

4. If your adolescent, nearly adult daughter wanted to know what your "core belief" about God is, how would you sum up your relationship with Christ—without preaching or quoting Scripture—in a single, personalized statement?

5. After reading 1 Corinthians 13:4–8, explain what it means to you in your own words.

Friends

There is a wisdom of the head, and . . .
a wisdom of the heart.

—*Charles Dickens*

Chapter Nine

———— 🙰 ————

Dear Mom,

I've wanted to write this letter to you for a long, long time, though I don't plan to ever send it. Since I'm uncomfortable saying these things to you in person, it seemed like a good idea to go ahead and get them out on paper. (Why is it that I'm so afraid of hurting you when you don't seem to care about saying and doing things that hurt me?)

Mom, all of my life I've wanted to have a closer relationship with you. Yet, for some reason, it never happens. I realize that it isn't fair to compare other families with ours, but I can't help it. When I'm with Angela and her mom, I notice how much fun they have together. They talk openly about things and laugh a lot. Mrs. Simmons really listens when Angie talks. I've never heard her criticize, put down, or make fun of her daughter. I like the way she praises my friend, the way her face lights up when Angie walks into the room, the way she speaks about her daughter with admiration, understanding, and respect. I can tell that she's really proud of her.

I wish we could be friends, Mom—the way Angie and her mother are. I wish you treated me the way Mrs. Simmons treats Angie. I hear you tell me that you love me, but you don't think to ask how I'm really doing most of the time, nor do you seem to care when I'm struggling. Maybe it's because you're usually centered on yourself and the personal struggles you are going through. I feel resentful when you expect me to listen endlessly to your problems without asking about how my life is going. You talk at me rather than with me. It makes me feel that you expect me to be someone different from who I actually am. Do you really know who I am? Am I someone worth cherishing with the best that you have to offer? Can you love me without a long list of conditions attached? I don't know.

Perhaps I'm being unrealistic, Mom. Lots of my friends feel frustrated, angry, or sad about their mothers. Perhaps I'm expecting too much from you. It's hard to imagine that you'll ever offer me the kind of care that I would like to receive from you, my mother. You are the way you are, period. And I just need to accept it.

As long as we don't have to be around one another very often, I can live with our relationship as it is. I have other friends to fill in the gap that has been created by your absence. But I'll always miss you, Mom—because I love you.

Yours truly,

Candace

Sowing and Reaping

Unmet expectations. Competing demands. Hurt feelings. Frustrated hopes. Harsh words. Broken communication. The feeling that you can't see me . . . that you aren't listening . . . that you just don't care.

Candace had experienced all of these things with her mother before she tearfully sat down with pen and paper at her dorm-room desk. Her intense feelings of sadness, rejection, anger, and deep disappointment are familiar to any girl or woman who longs for a healthy mother-daughter bond.

But it doesn't have to be this way. We can choose not to engage in the destructive behaviors, beliefs, actions, and attitudes that harm our relationships with our daughters. By following the advice of what women say has helped them produce an abundant harvest of mother-daughter friendship, we too can reap its manifold rewards:

• *Nurture your daughter*

—Cultivate her growth wisely and patiently, from the heart.

—Provide tolerant care and proper nourishment.

—Watch for warning signs of impending trouble.

—Whenever necessary, ward off pests.

• *Shelter your daughter*

—Carefully construct a well-designed place of refuge.

—Supply protective covering over vulnerable areas.

—Offer a safe haven that is durable enough to withstand the human equivalent of heat waves, hailstorms, floods, heavy frosts, and other potentially damaging climate changes.

Home is where one starts from.
—*T. S. ELIOT*

——— ✖ ———

Touched to the heart, Mrs. March could only stretch out her arms, as if to gather her children and grandchildren to herself, and say, with face and voice full of motherly love, gratitude, and humility,—"O, my girls, however long you may live, I can never wish you a greater happiness than this!"
—*LOUISA MAY ALCOTT*

——— ✖ ———

Mother darling, it is wonderful to meet and talk over everything and share and laugh and understand each other's situations as no one else can.
—*ANNE MORROW LINDBERGH*

• *Support your daughter*

—Hold up her dignity.

—Build upon a base of love and respect.

—Forgive offenses quickly.

—Maintain a steady position to prevent her new growth from falling, sinking, or slipping.

—Bear with her weaknesses.

• *Prune your life*

—Put God in charge of your spiritual training.

—Allow the Holy Spirit to trim the shape of your character.

—Be willing to let the Lord remove the unproductive parts of your life as He guides and promotes your growth.

—Cut back upon command: Learn to limit your outside activities and commitments as God leads.

Mother-daughter friendship flourishes with the nurture, shelter, and support that we give to our offspring. This friendship must be carefully tended, watered, weeded, and harvested. A certain amount of time is required to do these things well. It is not only a question of making the most of each moment, but also of making sure enough time is invested. Like a garden, a healthy mother-daughter bond cannot be created without our careful planning and cultivation. To build a lasting friendship with our daughters, we must be willing to spend quality time with them *in ample quantity*. A beautiful garden does not blossom instantly.

Jesus proclaimed, "For where your treasure is, there your heart will be also" (Matt. 6:21). Daughters know when they are treasured by their mothers. They can see it in our eyes, hear it in our voices, feel it in our touch, sense it in our presence. When we honor our daughters with our time, attention, and comfort, they know they are highly esteemed and sincerely valued. They understand why their feelings, passions, life experiences, and well-being matter to us. Above all, they trust that our love for them is nonnegotiable.

Making Memories Together

Think back to a time when a friend gave you the gift of her time, attention, and comfort. How did you feel? What did she do for you that was especially meaningful? Can you explain the particular qualities you most appreciated about her?

Our favorite friends know our likes and dislikes. Though they are familiar with our weaknesses, they choose to focus on our strengths. When they speak the truth to us in love, we usually listen.

And so it is with mothers. As we gently foster friendship with our daughters, we discover a host of practical ways to demonstrate our love for them while carefully considering their needs and paying attention to their personal preferences. "Compassion and knowing what *another* person needs comes through having been cared for," affirmed author Edith Schaeffer in *What Is a Family?* "Anyone who has had the comfort of a little pot of tea, some cookies or toast, or a cup of coffee and some cheese and crackers, or a glass of milk and some fruit—just when he was feeling 'down' in the midst of a project—then knows how to do the same things for someone else. A family is the place

"I did not have a mom that I could sit with and talk to about anything."
—DEBBIE, AGE 41

— ✺ —

A young branch takes on all the bends that one gives to it.
—CHINESE PROVERB

— ✺ —

May your father and mother be glad; may she who gave you birth rejoice!
—PROVERBS 23:25

— ✺ —

Repeated failures do little to inspire confidence. This is why we are called to forget the things that are behind. We must forget the failures. We must not wallow in defeat. We must press on toward the mark. We must never, never, never give up.
—R. C. SPROUL

where this kind of care should be so frequently given that it becomes natural to think of the needs of other people."[1]

Caring for one another's needs *does* come more naturally to us when we grow up in a family such as the one Edith Schaeffer described. When consistent family nurture is experienced on a daily basis throughout childhood, children are more likely to become healthy caregivers as adults. Those of us who did not receive tender caregiving will find ourselves spending more effort and determination learning it later in life. *With God's help, we can elect to learn better ways of caring for our own children and become the nurturing encouragers we were originally designed to be.* Serving our daughters, we find, models what it means to compassionately care for the needs of others.

Creating a place in which mother-daughter friendship can bloom also opens the door to sharing fruitful fellowship with the Savior. Making memorable moments with your daughter is an excellent place to start. Going to a favorite restaurant or coffee shop for breakfast or an early evening break, sharing afternoon tea, accompanying one another to the movies, taking trips, playing on the same softball team, and attending a play or concert are some of the activities that mothers and daughters say they especially enjoy doing together. In my experience, the times I share with my daughters just "getting away from it all" have provided unparalleled opportunities for prayer, informal talks about God, and discussions about the Bible. In this way, talking about Jesus and what we are learning in our walk with Him comes up frequently, as a natural part of our conversation.

When I spend time alone with one of my daughters, we usually do not have any set agenda. Often, we find it is easier to talk without distractions when we are away from the house, where ringing phones and competing voices frequently interrupt our conversation. We occasionally splurge on out-of-state travel, spend the night at a bed-and-breakfast near our home, or take a day trip to a small town located within easy driving distance. After making a hasty retreat to a nearby shopping mall for a mini-excursion, we may window shop and walk in climate-controlled comfort to our hearts' content when outdoor recreation is hampered by the weather. For the most part, our time together is determined by our schedules and energy levels and the amount of cash we have on hand.

My friend Shawn fondly remembered a time when she and her mom took a particularly meaningful vacation together without her siblings or father. The experience proved to be an unforgettable turning point in Shawn's relationship with her mother, Darlene.

"When I was in my twenties and she was in her forties, I took Mom camping on Oracoke Island off Cape Hatteras. During our trip, we drove hundreds of miles together and grew to know one another as adults," Shawn explained. "We had a pup tent. Since we had forgotten to bring the tent poles, however, we whittled wood to serve as makeshift sticks. Wading in the ocean while collecting shells with Mom was particularly pleasant, but when a storm with gale-force winds blew in, we momentarily wondered what we were doing there!"

Lasting Impressions

When asked to share their favorite memories of their mothers, women often recount seemingly small events that formed a clear and lasting impression of maternal care and comfort in their minds. Isn't it reassuring to realize that even the little things we do make a difference in our daughters' lives?

In the following examples, women of different ages looked back and remembered their most cherished mother-daughter scenes, reminding us that what we do *today* matters—perhaps even for a lifetime.

A friend loves at all times.
—PROVERBS 17:17A

— ❧ —

Love penetrates the defenses that have been built up to protect against rejection and scorn and belittlement, and it sees life created by God for love.
—EUGENE H. PETERSON

— ❧ —

If we are to trust God, we must learn to see that He is continuously at work in every aspect and every moment of our lives.
—JERRY BRIDGES

— ❧ —

The duties of home are discipline for the ministries of heaven.
—ANONYMOUS

"Coming home to the smell of cookies baking and . . . Mom was there. Always there. I knew she loved me. When I was sick as a child, my dad would tell me, 'No TV.' But, after he left for work, Mom would play cards with me ('Authors') and I'd always win! If I was nauseated and threw up, Mom would hold my forehead and sit with me, periodically wiping my face and refreshing me with ginger ale. One summer, between college terms, I went home for the entire summer, and Mom and I took turns doing Bible verses in Proverbs. It was so deep and refreshing."—Jana, age 32

"Camping in the summertime; games and homemade ice cream on the Fourth of July; Christmas caroling."

—Vonda, age 38

"Going for rides in the car, sharing, crying—just being together during the later years of Mom's life. When I was a teen, she played jokes on me. My mother was a fun person."

—Ann, age not given

"Going to the zoo, museums, parks—field trip excursions! Mom taught me to enjoy beauty, art, and music by spending time showing me these things."

—Shelley, age 25

"One-on-one time with my mom. Doing goofy things that made my mom laugh. That was really rewarding. I can remember her polishing my nails and stroking my hair late at night when I couldn't sleep. I think even as a young child I could sense a sadness in my mom. I was always very happy when she appeared to be having a good time."

—Linda, age 38

"Going to a beauty shop as a young girl and holding hands as we crossed the street together; Mom helping me pull up my tights; back-to-school shopping."

—Pam, age 27

"When I was growing up, my mother made most of my clothes. I hated it at the time, but now I cherish the memories of my mother at the sewing machine and of my having to stand still while she pinned up a hem. When I was in junior high, I wanted to walk home from school with my friends and my mother would come and pick up my alto saxophone so I wouldn't have to carry it."

—Donna, age 48

"Sharing while doing the dishes; praying together when I was hurting; crying on Mom's shoulder late at night; girl talks. And, yes, definitely *shopping."*

—Kelli, age 24

"My favorite memories include the times that we worked together on solving a sewing challenge or collaborating on some creative endeavor. They include the great moments we had shopping while we were looking for that special something. And I have warm, peaceful memories of the times that I went out to her house in the country to 'get away from it all.'"

—Bonnie, age 42

Looking Ahead

Mother-daughter friendship grows in stages, starting with the first moments of our daughters' lives. As it progresses through the trials of toddlerhood, the tribulations of puberty, and the testings of adolescence, we sometimes may wonder if it is ever going to

"Though my mom and I had a good relationship when I was growing up, it lacked a certain intimacy. It wasn't until I married and had a child that our relationship developed that intimacy."
—BONNIE, AGE 42

We must be kind to one another, tenderhearted, forgiving one another, even as God, for Christ's sake, has forgiven us.
—HANNAH WHITALL SMITH

Service is not a list of things that we do, though in it we discover things to do.
—RICHARD FOSTER

Kind words are the music of the world.
—FREDERICK WILLIAM FABER

develop at all. During dormant periods, prayer and patience may be the best way to keep the bond strong.

If you are going through a difficult time in your relationship with your daughter, do not despair. God knows the desires of your heart. He can mend the hurting places and rebuild broken relationships. No matter where you are on your mothering journey, Jesus offers you the hope of restoration and reconciliation as you walk with Him into the future. Will you trust the Lord to hear your prayers as you give your daughter to Him for His purposes and glory?

Mother-daughter friendship is a precious gift. Daughters who have received it from their mothers say that nothing else compares with the kind of nurturing comfort only their moms can supply. Mothers who have given it smile with genuine satisfaction when asked to describe what they like most about their relationships with their daughters. It is a friendship worth seeking and winning.

In closing, please pray with me for the daily grace and strength we *all* need to build and maintain a strong, healthy bond with our daughters:

> Dear Lord, we praise You for blessing us with the gift of our daughters. Raising them is a matchless privilege—we are humbled every day by the responsibilities of our calling! Our hearts are encouraged by knowing that You are making the journey with us, that we are not alone in our lifelong task, that Your Spirit is with us every step of the way.
>
> Help us, Lord! Send Your strength and wisdom. Forgive us when we fall short, restoring us quickly in Your holy presence. Grant us the grace to serve You with joy each day. May we be pleasing to You in all that we do, think, and say.
>
> Thank You, Father, for entrusting our daughters to our care and nurture. We place them as an offering before Your throne and dedicate them to You for Your eternal purposes and glory. Protect them from evil as You bring them to everlasting life through the salvation of Your Son, Jesus Christ. In His name we pray. Amen.

Revising the Script

The exercises below will aid you in making an assessment of mother-daughter relationships you have seen or read about over the years in fiction, the media, and Bible stories. To determine the impact that these and other maternal role models have had upon your life, you may want to consider the following categories:

1. FANTASY MOTHERS. From the perspective of most fairy tales, make-believe moms represent our worst nightmares about mothering, with wicked witches *(Snow White and the Seven Dwarfs)*, slave-driving stepmothers *(Cinderella)*, and abusive adults *(Hansel and Gretel)* leading the pack. In many childhood stories, the mother has passed away or is absent *(Beauty and the Beast, Bambi, The Little Mermaid, Rapunzel, The Chronicles of Narnia)*, with the daughter often being cared for by a surrogate parent—for example, Auntie Em *(The Wizard of Oz)*, Grandfather the Hermit *(Heidi)*, Miss Minchin *(The Little Princess)*, or a trio of forest fairies *(Sleeping Beauty)*. FOOD FOR THOUGHT: What do these stories say about the nature of mother-daughter relationships? How has fiction helped or hindered your understanding of the beauty—and desirability—of mother-daughter friendship?

2. MEDIA MOTHERS. Over the past 50 years, television programs have depicted mothers of every type, from the capable characters of the fifties and sixties—of these, June Cleaver *(Leave It to Beaver)*, Donna Baxter *(The*

Donna Reed Show), and Harriet Nelson *(Ozzie and Harriet)* are perhaps the most memorable—to the rule-breaking role models depicted several decades later on sitcoms such as *Roseanne* and *Married . . . with Children.* A few of the flesh-and-blood mothers portrayed in the media *(Eleni,* in particular, comes to mind here) offer unforgettable portrayals of maternal love. Ma Ingalls *(Little House on the Prairie),* Clair Huxtable *(The Bill Cosby Show),* Jill Taylor *(Home Improvement),* and others also inspire audiences as they are shown coping with family stress. FOOD FOR THOUGHT: Have you ever felt that your life was not measuring up to standards depicted in the media? Do you compare your relationship with your daughter to someone you have seen on TV or in a film? Which media mothers have shown positive, true-to-life portrayals of mother-daughter friendship? Of these, who is your favorite character? Why?

3. BIBLICAL MOTHERS. Browse through the Bible's lengthy list of mothers, from Eve to Eunice, looking specifically for examples of healthy mother-daughter friendships. If you reach the book of Revelation without locating a lengthy, in-depth description of mother-daughter friendship, don't be surprised. There isn't one. (Naomi must be excluded from consideration because she was Ruth's mother-in-law, not the woman who raised Ruth from the time of her birth.) Perhaps part of the reason for this lies in the fact that the Bible isn't fiction. Scripture does not show us glittery, idealized versions of family relationships like Hollywood does. It shares complex human stories in historic contrast to God's holiness and love, emphasizing every person's need for redemption by a compassionate Creator. The mothers we see in the Bible were not mythical creatures who were

incapable of misconduct—they were real people living in a fallen world. Like us, they were pulled in several directions at once and faced family-stress overload. FOOD FOR THOUGHT: When you read the stories about mothers in the Bible, which women stand out? Why? What have you learned from their examples?

4. SPIRITUAL MOTHERS. Elizabeth, Mary's companion during three months of her pregnancy with Jesus, presents an excellent example of spiritual mothering from a biblical perspective. In the word picture given in Luke 1:42–45, we capture a glimpse of the lasting value of a friendship ordained and blessed by God. Elizabeth's remarkable gifts to Mary—affirmation, support, service, faith, encouragement, hospitality, humility, respect, hope, and an open heart—challenge us to offer God's best to our daughters. FOOD FOR THOUGHT: Have you ever had a "spiritual mother" who gave any of these gifts to you? In your journal, describe what this experience was like and what it meant to you. After considering Elizabeth's example, is there anything you would like to add to your own mother-daughter friendship? What would you do differently?

5. Now that you have finished reading *Kindred Hearts,* review the letter-writing exercise at the end of chapter 1. Reread the letters you wrote, thinking through any changes you would like to make, revising as needed. When you have finished, write a letter or a prayer to God expressing the desires of your heart about your relationships with your mother and daughter, then seal it in an envelope for future reference.

Notes

Chapter 1

1. Katherine Trevelyan, quoted in Helen Exley, *Mother's Notebook* (New York: Exley, 1990), 11.

Chapter 3

1. Statistics quoted in Debra Evans, *Beauty and the Best* (Colorado Springs, Colo.: Focus on the Family, 1993). Taken from Mark Muro, "A New Era of Eros in Advertising," *The Boston Globe*, 16 Apr. 1986, and Jeffrey Zaslow, "Fourth-Grade Girls These Days Ponder Weighty Matters," *The Wall Street Journal*, 11 Feb. 1986.
2. Oswald Chambers, *Daily Thoughts for Disciples* (Grand Rapids: Zondervan, 1976), 95.

Chapter 5

1. Data taken from *The New York Times*, Nov. 1983. Cited in Kurt Haas and Adelaide Haas, *Understanding Sexuality* (St. Louis: Times Mirror/Mosby, 1987), 157.
2. William Law, quoted in *The Joy of the Saints*, edited by Robert L. Llewelyn (Springfield, Ill.: Templegate, 1988), 66.
3. James Houston, *The Transforming Power of Prayer* (Colorado Springs, Colo.: NavPress, 1996), 78.

4. Francis de Sales, quoted in *The Wisdom of the Saints,* edited by Jill Haak Adels (Oxford: Oxford University Press, 1987), 39.
5. Oswald Chambers, *Daily Thoughts for Disciples* (Grand Rapids: Zondervan, 1976), 291.

Chapter 6
1. Prayer by Reinhold Niebuhr, 1934. Cited in John Bartlett, *Familiar Quotations,* 16th ed., Justin Kaplan, general editor (Boston: Little, Brown, 1992), 684.
2. Quoted in *The Christian's Treasury of Stories and Songs, Prayers and Poems, and Much More for Young and Old,* edited and compiled by Lissa Roche (Wheaton, Ill.: Crossway, 1995), 86.

Chapter 7
1. Ingrid Trobisch, *The Joy of Being a Woman* (New York: Harper & Row, 1975).
2. Katherine W. Pettis and R. Dave Hughes, "Sexual Victimization of Children: A Current Perspective," *Behavioral Disorders* (Feb. 1985):137; Marianne Neifert, *Dr. Mom: A Guide to Baby and Child Care* (New York: Signet, 1986), 438–39.
3. Dan B. Allender, *The Wounded Heart: Hope for Adult Victims of Childhood Sexual Abuse* (Colorado Springs, Colo.: NavPress, 1990), 30.
4. Ibid., 33.
5. Taken from parenting-class materials provided by the Lincoln Police Department, Lincoln, Neb., 1984.
6. Stanton L. Jones and Brenna B. Jones, *How and When to Tell Your Kids About Sex* (Colorado Springs, Colo.: NavPress, 1993), 10.

Chapter 8
1. Mother Teresa, quoted in Malcolm Muggeridge, *Something Beautiful for God* (San Francisco: Perennial/Harper & Row, 1986), 68.

2. John Bosco, quoted in *The Wisdom of the Saints,* edited by Jill Haak Adels (Oxford: Oxford University Press, 1987), 103.
3. Hannah Whitall Smith, *The Christian's Secret of a Happy Life* (Old Tappan, N.J.: Fleming H. Revell, 1986), 26.

Chapter 9
1. Edith Schaeffer, *What Is a Family?* (Old Tappan, N.J.: Fleming H. Revell, 1975), 86.

Bibliography

Abrams, M. H., ed. *The Norton Anthology of English Literature.* New York: Norton, 1987.

Adels, Jill Haak, ed. *The Wisdom of the Saints.* Oxford: Oxford University Press, 1987.

Allender, Dan B. *The Wounded Heart: Hope for Adult Victims of Childhood Sexual Abuse.* Colorado Springs, Colo.: NavPress, 1990.

Appleton, George, ed. *The Oxford Book of Prayer.* Oxford: Oxford University, 1985.

Bennett, William J., ed. *The Moral Compass.* New York: Simon & Schuster, 1995.

Bigliardi, Patricia A. *Beyond the Hidden Pain of Abortion.* Lynnwood, Wash.: Aglow, 1994.

Bonhoeffer, Dietrich. *The Martyred Christian.* Ed. Joan Winmill Brown. New York: Macmillan, 1983.

Bridges, Jerry. *Trusting God.* Colorado Springs, Colo.: NavPress, 1988.

Briscoe, Jill, and Stuart Briscoe. *Songs from Heaven and Earth.* Nashville: Thomas Nelson, 1985.

Carder, Dave, Henry Cloud, John Townsend et al. *Secrets of Your Family Tree*. Chicago: Moody, 1991.

Chambers, Oswald. *My Utmost for His Highest*. New York: Dodd, Mead, 1935.

Dillard, Annie. *Pilgrim at Tinker Creek*. New York: Bantam, 1975.

Dobson, James C. *Life on the Edge*. Dallas: Word, 1995.

——————. *Preparing for Adolescence*. Ventura, Calif.: Vision, 1980.

Dobson, James C., and Gary Bauer. *Children at Risk: The Battle for the Hearts and Minds of Our Children*. Dallas: Word, 1992.

Edelman, Hope. *Motherless Daughters: The Legacy of Loss*. Reading, Mass.: Addison-Wesley, 1994.

Ells, Alfred. *Restoring Innocence: Healing the Memories and Hurts That Hinder Sexual Intimacy*. Nashville: Thomas Nelson, 1990.

Evans, Debra. *Beauty and the Best: A Christian Woman's Guide to True Beauty*. Colorado Springs, Colo.: Focus on the Family, 1993.

——————. *Women of Character: Life-Changing Examples of Godly Women*. Grand Rapids: Zondervan, 1996.

Foster, Richard. *Celebration of Discipline*. New York: Harper & Row, 1978.

——————. *Prayers from the Heart*. San Francisco: HarperSanFrancisco, 1994.

Houston, James. *The Transforming Power of Prayer*. Colorado Springs, Colo.: NavPress, 1996.

Hudson, Robert R., and Shelley Townsend-Hudson. *Companions for the Soul*. Grand Rapids: Zondervan, 1995.

Hull, Karen. *The Mommy Book: Advice to New Mothers from Those Who've Been There.* Grand Rapids: Zondervan, 1986.

Hunter, Brenda. *What Every Mother Should Know.* Sisters, Ore.: Multnomah, 1993.

Johnson, Barbara. *Splashes in the Cesspools of Life.* Dallas: Word, 1992.

Johnson, Greg, and Susie Shellenberger. *Getting Ready for the Guy/Girl Thing: Two Ex-Teenagers Reveal the Shocking Truth About God's Plan for Success with the Opposite Sex.* Ventura, Calif.: Regal, 1991.

Johnson, Greg, and Mike Yorkey. *Faithful Parents, Faithful Kids.* Wheaton, Ill.: Tyndale House, 1993.

Jones, Stanton L., and Brenna B. Jones. *How and When to Tell Your Kids About Sex.* Colorado Springs, Colo.: NavPress, 1993.

Keyes, Dick. *Beyond Identity: Finding Your Self in the Character and Image of God.* Ann Arbor: Servant, 1984.

Kuykendall, Carol. *Give Them Wings.* Colorado Springs, Colo.: Focus on the Family, 1994.

Lewis, C. S. *George MacDonald: An Anthology.* New York: Macmillan, 1974.

Lindbergh, Anne Morrow. *Gift from the Sea.* New York: Random House, 1975.

Lindskoog, Kathryn. *Around the Year with C. S. Lewis and His Friends: A Book of Days.* Norwalk, Conn.: Gibson, 1986.

Llewelyn, Robert, ed. *The Joy of the Saints.* Springfield, Ill.: Templegate, 1988.

Macaulay, Susan Schaeffer. *Something Beautiful for God.* Westchester, Ill.: Crossway, 1980.

McDowell, Josh. *Sex, Guilt, and Forgiveness.* Wheaton, Ill.: Tyndale House, 1990.

Mains, Karen Burton. *With My Whole Heart: Disciplines for Strengthening the Inner Life.* Portland, Ore.: Multnomah, 1987.

Marshner, Connie. *Decent Exposure: How to Teach Your Children About Sex.* Franklin, Tenn.: Legacy Communications, 1994.

Mayo, Mary Ann. *God's Good Gift: Teaching Your Kids About Sex—Ages 8 to 11.* Grand Rapids: Zondervan, 1991.

Mead, Frank S., ed. *12,000 Religious Quotations.* Grand Rapids: Baker, 1989.

Mother Teresa. *A Gift for God.* New York: Harper & Row, 1975.

Muggeridge, Malcolm. *Something Beautiful for God.* San Francisco: Perennial/Harper & Row, 1986.

Peterson, Eugene H. *Earth and Altar: The Community of Prayer in a Self-Bound Society.* Downer's Grove, Ill.: InterVarsity, 1985.

Powell, John. *Will the Real Me Please Stand Up?* Allen, Tex.: Tabor, 1985.

Reimer, Kathie. *1001 Ways to Help Your Child Walk with God.* Wheaton, Ill.: Tyndale House, 1994.

Rekers, George, ed. *Family Building: Six Qualities of a Strong Family.* Ventura, Calif.: Regal, 1985.

Roche, Lissa, ed. and comp. *The Christian's Treasury of Stories and Songs, Prayers and Poems, and Much More for Young and Old.* Wheaton, Ill.: Crossway, 1995.

Schaeffer, Edith. *What Is a Family?* Old Tappan, N.J.: Fleming H. Revell, 1975.

Shaver, Jessica. *Gianna Aborted . . . and Lived to Tell About It.* Colorado Springs, Colo.: Focus on the Family, 1995.

Smalley, Gary. *The Key to Your Child's Heart.* Dallas: Word, 1992.

————. *The Key to Your Teenager's Heart.* Dallas: Word, 1995.

Smedes, Lewis B. *The Art of Forgiving: When You Need to Forgive and Don't Know How.* Nashville: Moorings, 1996.

————. *Sex for Christians: The Limits and Liberties of Sexual Living.* Grand Rapids: Eerdmans, 1976.

Smith, Hannah Whitall. *The Christian's Secret of a Happy Life.* Old Tappan, N.J.: Fleming H. Revell, 1986.

Sproul, R. C. *Pleasing God.* Wheaton, Ill.: Tyndale, 1988.

Stephens, Andrea, and Bill Stephens. *Prime Time: Devotions for Girls.* Grand Rapids: Fleming H. Revell, 1992.

Sterling, Beth. *The Thorn of Sexual Abuse: The Gripping Story of a Family's Courage and One Man's Struggle.* Grand Rapids: Fleming H. Revell, 1994.

Stone, Bob, and Bob Palmer. *The Dating Dilemma: Handling Sexual Pressures.* Grand Rapids: Baker Book House, 1990.

Stott, John. *Involvement: Social and Sexual Relationships in the Modern World.* Old Tappan, N.J.: Fleming H. Revell, 1985.

Teresa of Avila. *The Collected Works of St. Teresa of Avila.* Trans. Kieran Kavanaugh and Otilio Rodriguez. Washington, D.C.: ICS Publications, 1976.

Trobisch, Ingrid. *The Joy of Being a Woman.* New York: Harper & Row, 1975.

Trobisch, Walter. *Love Is a Feeling to Be Learned.* Downer's Grove, Ill.: InterVarsity, 1971.

Weber, Linda. *Mom, You're Incredible!* Colorado Springs, Colo.: Focus on the Family, 1994.

Welter, Paul. *How to Help a Friend.* Wheaton, Ill.: Tyndale, 1978.

Wesley, John. *The Gift of Love.* Ed. Arthur Skevington. London: Darton, Longman, and Todd, 1988.

White, Joe. *Faith Training.* Colorado Springs, Colo.: Focus on the Family, 1994.

Wordsworth, William. *The Poems.* London: Penguin, 1989.

Yates, Elizabeth. *A Book of Hours.* New York: Walker, 1985.

Zimmerman, Martha. *Should I Keep My Baby?* Minneapolis: Bethany House, 1983.